11 Plus GL Verbal Reasoning Workbook

Published: achieve2day, Slough, 2019

ISBN: 978-1-909986-48-0

Contents

Chapter 1: Letters

1.1 Letter Sequences

To continue a sequence you need to work out the pattern. The pattern can go forwards or backwards in the alphabet. Use the alphabet at the top of the page to help you. Always write down your working out, use '+' for going forwards and '-' for going backwards. The alphabet is treated like a continuous circle where A follows Z and Z is immediately before A.

Example 1: B D F H J ___ ___

In this example when we look at the difference between letters.

B $^{+2}$ D $^{+2}$ F $^{+2}$ H $^{+2}$ J ___ ___

Each of the letters go forward two, so the next letter will also be 'add two,' which is 'L.' Then a further two letters is 'N.'

Example 2: B Y V S P ___ ___

In this example when we look at the difference between letters

B $^{-3}$ Y $^{-3}$ V $^{-3}$ S $^{-3}$ P ___ ___

Each of the letters go backwards three, so the next letter will also be 'minus three,' which is 'M.' Then the three letters before M is 'J.' Notice how three letters before B is Y.

Exercise 1.1

Write the next two letters in these letter sequences.

1. C F I L O ___ ___
2. T X B F J ___ ___
3. K I G E C ___ ___
4. M H C X S ___ ___
5. Q S U W Y ___ ___

Sometimes the difference between letters changes, according to a pattern.

Example 3: A B D G K ___ ___

In this example is we look at the difference between letters.

$A^{+1} B^{+2} D^{+3} G^{+4} K$ ___ ___

The letters go forward be 1, 2, 3, 4. So they are going forward by one more each time. Next will be 'add 5' so the letter is 'P'. Then it will be 'add 6', so the final letter is 'V'.

Example 4: A B D E G ___ ___

In this example is we look at the difference between letters.

$A^{+1} B^{+2} D^{+1} E^{+2} G$ ___ ___

The letters go forward be 1, 2, 1, 2. So they are going alternating between adding one and two. Next one is added, so the answer is 'H'. Then two is added, so the second letter is 'J'.

Now try these:

6.	A	D	F	I	K	___	___
7.	K	M	L	N	M	___	___
8.	Y	S	N	J	G	___	___
9.	Y	B	F	I	M	___	___
10.	T	W	V	Y	X	___	___

W X Y Z A B C D E F G H I J K L M N O P Q R S T U V W X Y Z A B C D

Usually, the letters are in pairs and the first number and second number need to be treated separately.

Example 5: AV CU ET GS ___

If you look at the difference between the first letter in each pair, you get:

AV $^{+2}$ CU $^{+2}$ ET $^{+2}$ GS ___

Two is added each time so the first letter of the next pair will be G add two which is I.

If we look at the difference between the second letter of each pair and write it in below, we get:

AV $^{+2}{}_{-1}$ CU $^{+2}{}_{-1}$ ET $^{+2}{}_{-1}$ GS ___

For the second letter we go back one each time, so the second letter of the next pair will be S minus one which is R.

This can be written as individual letters but we 'leapfrog' and look at alternate letters.

Now try these:

11. A M C K E I ___ ___
12. PN SP VR YT ___ ___
13. AD BF CH DJ ___ ___
14. AD DG GJ JM ___ ___
15. BZ BX CV ET ___ ___

Here is a mix of the above types:

16. AB BC CD DE ___ ___
17. AB CD EF GH ___ ___
18. BA ZY XW VU ___ ___
19. KR LU NY QD ___ ___
20. GG FJ DM AP ___ ___

1.2 Analogies

In analogies the relationship between the second pair must be exactly the ***same*** as the first pair. However, there doesn't need to be any connection between the two pairs.

Example 1. AC → BA as MP → ___

Looking at the first letter A → B you add one, so in the second pair you do exactly the ***same*** and add one giving 'N.' Then looking at the second letter C→ A you take two so for the second pair you do exactly the ***same*** and P minus two gives 'N.'

Therefore, AC → BA as MP → NN

Now try these:

1. AB → DE as MN → PQ
2. AC → EF as PR → TU
3. RP → NL as JH → FD
4. RT → SW as GI → HL
5. CD → GF as OP → SR
6. PO → LM as HI → dg
7. DD → FB as ZZ → BX
8. PR → SU as VX → YA
9. BC → ZA as KL → IJ
10. MN → NM as FG → GF

1.3 Order of Size

In these questions you need to rank the items in order of size or logical order and then underline the word that is in the correct position.

It is best to number all the words as it is easy, particularly in a stressful exam situation, to miss one. If you number them all you will notice if you skipped one, and can then go back and correct it. Otherwise it may remain missed out.

Example: Underline the one that comes in the middle if ordered according to size.

town	continent	house	country	county

First number in order of size.

2	5	1	4	3
town	continent	house	country	county

There are five items so the third would be in the middle. The third item, 'county' is underlined.

2	5	1	4	3
town	continent	house	country	<u>county</u>

Now try these:

Underline the middle word.

1.	3	5	4	2	1
2.	thirteen	fifteen	fourteen	twelve	eleven
3.	7:00 a.m.	9:00 p.m.	6:00 p.m.	11:00 a.m.	3:00 p.m.
4.	cold	hot	warm	freezing	boiling
5.	year 1	year 3	year 7	reception	nursery

Underline the second word.

6.	gigantic	tiny	medium	small	large
7.	good	worst	bad	best	better
8.	hundreds	units	tens	millions	thousands
9.	London	Big Ben	Europe	England	United Kingdom
10.	elephant	zebra	cat	ant	mouse

1.4 Alphabet Letters

Use the alphabet on the top of the page to answer these questions. Most involve counting letters.

The vowels are 'a', 'e', 'i', 'o' and 'u'. The consonants are all the other letters. You need to know which letters are vowels.

Now try these:

1. What is the sixth letter of the alphabet?
2. If the alphabet was written backwards what would be the second letter?
3. What is the first vowel?
4. What is the third vowel?
5. What letter appears twice in significant, once in concrete but not at all in glass?
6. What letter appears twice in better, once in worse but not at all in good.
7. What two letters appears in the words minute, tiny and little.
   Make a word from them.
8. The same two letters appear in the words; morning, evening and inside
   Make a word from them.
9. What is the consonant found in the word 'out'?
10. Which two letters are in the middle on the alphabet?

1.5 Practice

1.	FL	GJ	HH	IF	JD	____	____
2.	RG	QI	PK	OM	NO	____	____
3.	DH	FG	HF	JE	LD	____	____
4.	AG	AZ	BT	DO	GK	____	____
5.	RD	SG	UI	XL	BN	____	____

6.	AB → CD	as	MN →	____
7.	ST → RR	as	LK →	____
8.	II → GK	as	PP →	____
9.	FE → HG	as	VU →	____
10.	FI → CG	as	WY →	____

Underline the middle item, when arranged in order.

11.	sentence	letter	word	paragraph	chapter
12.	six	four	seven	five	eight
13.	second	third	first	fifth	fourth
14.	February	March	January	May	April
15.	hour	minute	day	month	week

16. What is the eighth letter of the alphabet? ____
17. If the alphabet was written backwards what would the fifth letter be? ____
18. What is the fourth vowel? ____
19. What letter appears twice in moon but not at all in sun? ____
20. What consonant appears in the word sea? ____

Chapter 2: Words

2.1 Finish and Start

In these questions you need to find a letter that finishes the first word and starts the second. It must be the same letter for both pairs of words.

If you cannot see a letter easily go through the alphabet from A to Z.

Example: rai( )eed clea( )eat

You could put a 'd' in the first set of words rai(d)eed to make the words raid and deed. However, clead is not a word so you need to find a different letter. 'N' works for both sets of words.

rai(n)eed clea(n)eat

with 'n' we make the words rain, need, clean and neat.

Now try these:

1.	clow( )ame	faste( )ote
2.	flowe( )iver	builde( )ain
3.	far( )ate	proble( )ess
4.	spIl ( )amp	bal( )ight
5.	pla( )oung	exactl( )ellow
6.	lon( )reat	flIn( )oat
7.	hal( )riend	gol( )ree
8.	firs( )est	faul( )race
9.	boar( )ark	crow( )oor
10.	loa ( )rog	cal( )eel

2.2 Alphabetic Order

To put words in alphabetic order, look at the first letter of each word and see which one comes closest to the beginning of the alphabet. Then which one comes second closest. Continue until you have ordered all the words.

Example 1: dog rat cat bat pig

The first letters are d, r, c, b, p. 'B' is the closest to the beginning of the alphabet so 'bat' is the first word. Of the remaining letters 'c' is the closest to the beginning of the alphabet, so 'cat' is next. We continue with the other words and the order is:

bat, cat, dog, pig, rat

If we were asked to underline a particular word, we could order them by writing small numbers above the words, like this:

3	5	2	1	4
dog	rat	cat	bat	pig

If we had been asked to underline the word which would come second we would underline the word 'cat'.

3	5	2	1	4
dog	rat	<u>cat</u>	bat	pig

Now try these:

Underline the word which would come third if placed in alphabetic order.

1. pear apple orange mandarin nectarine
2. book novel dictionary encyclopaedia cookbook
3. blue red green yellow orange
4. water cordial juice squash drink
5. present gift birthday candles music

If the first two letters are the same you need to look at the second letter. If the second letters are the same you need to look at the third letter. Whenever two letters are the same look at the next letter. The end of a word comes before another letter, so pen is before pencil.

Example 2: beech beach bench bee bent

They all start with 'B' so look at the next letter. The second letter is all 'E' so look at the third letter. The third letter is 'A', two 'E' and two 'N.' 'A' comes before 'E' or 'N' so 'beach' is the first word. 'Bee' is a whole word so that is second and 'beech' is third. Finally the N's. The fourth letter is 'C' or 'T.' 'C' comes before 'T' so 'bench' is fourth and 'bent' last.

3	1	4	2	5
beech	beach	bench	bee	bent

Now try these:

Underline the word which would come third if placed in alphabetic order.

6. potato pea parsnip pumpkin plum
7. glass games gentle gulp groove
8. person painter priest porter pilot
9. lot line luggage length land
10. order orchestra oregano ornate original

2.3 Missing Letters

In these questions the word in capitals is missing three letters which form a three letter word. Work out what the word in capitals should be. Then write the three letter word, only on the line.

It can help to write out the missing word and then underline the letters you already have.

Example. Tanuja's favourite fruit is STBERRIES

The sentence should read "Tanuja's favourite fruit is ST^{RAW}BERRIES," so the missing letters are RAW and 'raw' is the answer.

Now try these:

1. They took their visitor SIGHTING in London. _______
2. A PENON is a five sided shape with straight sides. _______
3. The boy liked doing JIG puzzles. _______
4. An octopus has eight TACLES. _______
5. Being chased by a monster was a TERLE experience. _______
6. Of all the insects in his collection the GRASSPER was his favourite. _______
7. She couldn't walk, so she used a WHEELCH. _______
8. The SHEPD looks after the sheep. _______
9. The mother's REION to the emergency was very quick. _______
10. It was a DISADTAGE not to have played the game before. _______

2.4 Hidden Words

In these questions a four letter word is hidden across at least two words. The easiest way to do these questions is to look briefly. If you can't see the word immediately use your fingers to frame the last three letters of the first word and the first letter of the second word. Then move your fingers across the sentence, one letter at a time, until you reach the word; because it is framed by your fingers it will be more obvious.

Example. Luke in a rush opened his presents.

Starting with fingers over the 'L' and 'N' 'ukei' is framed.

uke i a rush opened his presents.

The fingers move across until

Luke in a r sh op ned his presents.

And the word 'shop' is framed.

Now try these:

1.	The cone edge was moist with ice-cream.	______
2.	Hush in the library, the librarian reminded them.	______
3.	We had to wait until later, to play monopoly.	______
4.	The ranger checks hippopotamuses every day.	______
5.	The truth emerged slowly.	______
6.	Colic kept the baby awake.	______
7.	The idea required planning	______
8.	The serve by the tennis player was another ace.	______
9.	The child was polite and kind.	______
10.	His grandmother put a stitch in the bear's paw to fix it.	______

2.5 *Practice*

Write the letter in brackets that completes both sets of words.

1.	shir( )itle	Augus( )able
2.	boo( )ettle	floc( )itten
3.	dinosau( )ead	alte( )eason
4.	hurr( )oung	carefull( )esterday
5.	yout( )otel	searc( )ammer

Underline the word that would come fourth if placed in alphabetic order.

6.	engineer	doctor	builder	lawyer	teacher
7.	cakes	biscuits	muffins	slices	flans
8.	science	English	maths	history	geography
9.	money	machine	milk	meal	mug
10.	goat	glue	gym	gate	giant

Write the three letter word missing from the word in capitals.

11. At school COMING was his favourite subject. ______
12. At the end of the sports day the school CPION was announced. ______
13. The young couple were ENGD to be married. ______
14. The child was allowed to play when their homework was COMPE. ______
15. The child found their toy BENH the bed. ______

Underline the four letter word hidden in these sentences.

16. Please, can I reach into the box? ______
17. Look India is just here on the globe. ______
18. The double bass entered from the left. ______
19. The talent show entrants were very nervous. ______
20. The deadline arrived very quickly. ______

Chapter 3: Similar and Different

3.1 Odd Two Out

In these questions three of the words are connected in some way. Find the two words that do not go with these three and underline them.

Example 1: minute clock hour second time

Minute, hour and second are all units of time but clock and time are not. So clock and time are underlined. Note that the other words are related but not in the same way.

minute clock hour second time

Example 2: mum dad aunt uncle niece

Mum, aunt and niece are all female while dad and uncle are male. So dad and uncle are underlined.

mum dad aunt uncle niece

Now try these:

1. blue green rainbow red colour
2. dress skirt clothes shirt hands
3. water rice juice pasta cordial
4. foot ball hand racquet arm
5. flower house vegetables kitchen fruit
6. reading novel dictionary writing encyclopaedia
7. cow hen deer sheep duck
8. hospital patient heart liver kidney
9. candle lamp lightbulb telephone electricity
10. jam bread marmalade toast honey

3.2 *Synonyms*

In these questions two words have the same or similar meaning. To work out which words are similar, put one word in a sentence, if the word can be replaced with the second word and the sentence continues to mean the same thing, then that word is the answer.

Example: Which word is most similar to kind? happy, type, nice

Type is the most similar. We can put kind in a sentence "A Labrador is a kind of dog," then replace the word kind with type and we get "A Labrador is a type of dog." The sentence means the same thing.

You need to be careful of words like kind that have two (or more) meanings. Also, consider the type of word, for example: noun, verb, adjective and adverb.

Now try these:

Underline the word in brackets most similar to the first word.

1. Chuckle (smile, giggle joke)
2. Misfortune (difficult, ill, fail)
3. Happy (dancing, sad, pleased)
4. Icy (freezing, ice-cream, cold)
5. Enlarge (exaggerate, magnify, curtail)

Underline one word from each set of brackets with a similar meaning.

6. (intelligent, computer, memory) (stupid, clever, robot)
7. (table, chair, desk) (cupboard, bench, seat)
8. (spectacles, glasses, reading) (optician, tumblers, mirror)
9. (add, division, multiply) (remove, sum, some)
10. (make, brand, type) (card, create, sew)

Underline the word in brackets most similar to the first word.

11. Abide (bear, greet, join)
12. Rogue (leave, red, scamp)
13. Suppose (prove, assume, decide)
14. Fragile (break, robust, frail)
15. Distinct (clear, far, distance)

Underline one word from each set of brackets with a similar meaning.

16. (mean, kind, thoughtful) (angry, type, classify)
17. (buoyant, feeling, friendly) (water, cheerful, wistful)
18. (law, eyes, illicit) (forbidden, opticians, rude)
19. (glimpse, nothing, celebrity) (remove, stare, glance)
20. (wet, fine, sunny) (weather, well, water)

3.3 *Antonyms*

In this type of question you need to work out which words are opposites.

Example. 1: Underline the word from each group that are opposites.

(top, side, edge) (lid, bottom, best)

top and bottom are opposites, so they are underlined.

Now try these:

Underline the word in brackets which is opposite to the word in front.

1. Fraction (part, half, all)
2. Precise (correct, ambiguous, change)
3. Black (white, grey, orange)
4. Happy (unwell, angry, down)
5. Interior (house, outside, within)

Underline one word from each set of brackets with opposite meanings.

6. (present, gift, time) (birthday, now, past)
7. (write, wrong, right) (mark, left, grade)
8. (talk, hear, mouth) (cry, listen, ear)
9. (little, few, small) (tiny, many, amount)
10. (meal, dinner, food) (lunch, eat, drink)

Underline the word in brackets which is opposite to the word in front.

11. Abbreviate (curtail, reduce, prolong)
12. Construct (demolish, dislocate, fabricate)
13. Fade (vanish, flourish, high)
14. Finale (begin, opening, bow)
15. Rotten (putrid, pure, fresh)

Underline one word from each set of brackets with opposite meanings.

16. (cluster, insight, order) (control, throng, isolate)
17. (steep, ground, wash) (soil, even, rinse)
18. (attempt, attack, deter) (ignore, charge, repel)
19. (chutney, jam, jar) (squash, squeeze, clear)
20. (maroon, red, sad) (blue, rescue, choose)

3.4 *Middle Words*

In this type of question, there are two words. You need to put a word in the middle so that only one letter changes each time.

Example 1. L A S T

______

C A S E

Firstly, notice which two letters are already the same. These must stay the same. So 'A' and 'S' will remain.

L A S T
A S
C A S E

Then change either of the other letters to that of the final word. In our example if we change the final 'T' to an 'E' we get 'LASE' which is not a word, so we need to change 'L' to 'C' forming 'CAST.'

L A S T
C A S T
C A S **E**

Notice only one letter changes each time.

Now try these:

1. S H O E

   ______

   S N O W

2. R A R E

   ______

   H A R D

3. F L O W

   ______

   G R O W

4. C A N E

   ______

   C A R D

5. S O M E

   ______

   C O M B

6. P A I N

   ______

   F A I R

7. T O O K

   ______

   C O R K

8. B I N D

   ______

   M I N E

9. T O N E

   ______

   S O R E

10. P I N E

    ______

    L I M E

3.5 Practice

Underline the two words which do not fit with the other three

1. rose	tulip	tree	bush	lily
2. English	Maths	school	Science	classroom
3. lamb	sheep	horse	foal	piglet
4. swan	robin	mouse	eagle	badger
5. lady	gentleman	woman	girl	chap

Underline one word from each set of brackets with a similar meaning.

6. (scared, teased, sad)	(happy, frightened, cried)
7. (kind, dear, cheap)	(expensive, cost, content)
8. (rubbish, good, bad)	(tidy, joyful, litter)
9. (thick, narrow, size)	(wide, open, small)
10. (thick, wide, thin)	(heavy, slim, light)

Underline one word from each set of brackets with the opposite meaning.

11. (bad, naughty, rude)	(thoughtful, polite, caring)
12. (sleep, snore, bed)	(dream, run, awake)
13. (entrée, meal, dinner)	(dessert, main, desert)
14. (exercise, work, stop)	(today, start, new)
15. (child, old, family)	(young, teenager, father)

Find a word to go between the two given words so only one letter changes at a time.

16. D E A F

    ______

    G E A R

17. B A C K

    ______

    R A C E

18. B E A D

    ______

    R E A L

19. F L I P

    ______

    C H I P

20. L A N D

    ______

    B I N D

Chapter 4: Making Words

4.1 Can or Cannot be Made

In these questions the letters in the word can be used to form other words. It is as if the letters are scrabble tiles, the tiles are then moved around and you have to say whether words either can be made or not. Each letter can be used only once.

Example 1. Which word ***can be*** made from REFLECTION?

friend, lend, real, lent, sett

In this example we can't make 'friend' or 'lend' because we have no 'D,' or 'real' because we have no 'A,' or 'sett' because we only have one 'T' but 'sett' has two. However, we do have all the letters for 'lent' so that is our answer.

Now try these:

Underline the word which ***can be*** made from the word in capitals.

1. FARMER – mark, form, raft, fair, fare
2. DROPPED - droop, prod, popper, road, dread
3. LESSON - song, sonnet, lend, lent, lone
4. BETWEEN - neat, need, bean, went, bend
5. ALIGHT - tile, girl, hill, hail, grit

Underline the word which ***cannot be*** made from the word in capitals.

6. DICTIONARY - rain, yarn, dial, corn, radio
7. LEADERSHIP - peal, peel, seal, rain, pale
8. REASONING - song, gong, sear, near, nine
9. BRUSHED - bush, shrub, drum, rush, shed
10. SECOND - send, sent, cone, scone, dose

4.2 Compound Words

In these questions a word from the left can be joined to a word from the right to make a new word. The two words are underlined.

Example 1. (foot, leg, ankle) (time, step, stand)

The words foot and step can be written together to make footstep. So foot and step are underlined.

If you can't see the answer, start with the first word and put it with each word in the second set in turn. Then move to the second word in the first set and then the third word until you find two words which will go together.

Now try these:

1. (pass, press, ship) (dock, boat, port)
2. (box, sand, beach) (pen, paper, pencil)
3. (I, eye, jar) (top, lid, see)
4. (wrist, hand, foot) (sock, glove, shake)
5. (finger, pencil, paint) (tine, print, grip)

Sometimes, when the two words become one the pronunciation of the words change. Be aware that words ending in 't' or 's' if the next word starts with 'h' produces 'th' or 'sh.' Double letters such as 'oo' also change sound. Also, you need to be careful of spelling.

Example 2. (cup, saucer, plate) (bored, board, coaster)

In this example 'cup' and 'board' make 'cupboard.'

Now try these:

6. (is, so, in) (on, at, it)
7. (fat, fit, his) (turn, thin, her)
8. (sud, mud, read) (din, den, fish)
9. (batter, better, butter) (flew, flap, fly)
10. (cheque, check, stamp) (pet, up, down)

4.3 *Rearranging Words*

In these questions there are three pairs of words. You need to work out how the first two pairs work and then do ***exactly the same*** with the third pair.

Example 1. (share, hare) (stare, tare) (scone,)

To go from share to hare we remove the first letter, to go from stare to tare we remove the first letter. So for the third pair we ***do exactly the same*** and remove the first letter. So our answer is cone.

(share, hare) (stare, tare) (scone, **cone**)

Now try these:

1. (swan, swans) (tern, terns) (duck,)
2. (row, crow) (one, cone) (are,)
3. (blew, flew) (bare, fare) (bear,)
4. (ship, slip) (chap, clap) (chip,)
5. (sock, flock) (sake, flake) (sag,)

In this type of rearranging words, the word in brackets is made from the outside words. You must make the word in the middle of the second set of words in the same way as the first. To do this, number the middle word and then put those numbers over the letters of the outside words where they came from. Then use the same pattern, for the second set.

Example 2. b e a r [r a i n] i n t o   l e a f [   ] i r o n

In this example, the 'r' is from the last letter of bear, 'a' the second last letter of bear and 'i' and 'n' is from the first two letters of into. So we have:

```
    21  1234   34
bear [rain] into
```

Then we can put this pattern of numbering on the second set of words.

```
    21  1234   34
leaf [      ] iron
```

Then we can put fill in the middle bracket.

```
    21  1234   34
leaf [fair] iron
```

Now try these:

6. r i n d [d i c e] r a c e   c l a p [   ] d r u m

7. b o n e [b o a r] a r i d   s o a r [   ] m e n d

8. k n o t [t i n e] h e i r   u s e r [   ] v e i n

9. b a r n [d e a r] f e e d   k i l n [   ] b a i t

10. l o s t [c o l t] a c h e   s o m e [   ] a r c h

Often, in these questions a letter may have more than one possibility.

Example 3: (sweet, wet) (story, try) (types,)

Answer: For the first set of brackets, the 'e' is the middle of wet could come from either the third or fourth letter of sweet. So start with the second set of brackets. In the second set of brackets the second letter must come from the fourth letter. So the second word is made from the letters of the first word as follows:

```
 12345  245
(story,  try)
```

Going back to the first word, we can make wet using the 2, 4 and 5th letters of sweet. Whatever, we do for the first two pairs, for the third pair we do ***exactly the same***.

```
 12345  245   12345  245   12345  245
(sweet, wet) (story, try) (types, yes)
```

So the answer is 'yes'.

Example 4: h o o d [d o m e] m e n d   e a r l [   ] i r o n

Answer: We put the numbering above, the first set of words as before. However, if there are two possibilities we must make sure that we include both.

```
 2 2 1    1 2 3 4    3 4  1
h o o d [d o m e] m e n d
```

Then we number the second set of brackets and fill in the middle bracket, filling in the letters we know first.

```
 2 21    1 2 3 4   3 4  1
e a r l [      i r] i r o n
```

Then have a look at the letters that are duplicated. The first letter can be 'l' or 'n' and the second letter can be 'a' or 'r'. Write the possibilities down and look for a word.

```
 2 21    1 2 3 4    3 4  1
e a r l [ n a i r ] i r o n
          l r
```

Lair is a word, so that is the answer.

Now try these:

11. (tool, lot) (told, dot) (mild,)

12. (sands, sad) (binds, bid) (funny,)

13. (beef, fee) (veal, lea) (sows,)

14. (here, her) (capo, cop) (gale,)

15. (sensor, rose) (reload, dare) (unison,)

16. f a c e [c a l l] b e l l   c u f f [ ] m u l e

17. s o n g [n o s e] n a v e   s u r e [ ] f e e t

18. f o l d [g o l f] g o a l   t o n e [ ] r a y s

19. c o o k [c o l d] l e a d   f l i p [ ] n e e d

20. f a r e [l o a f] l o r e   m u c h [ ] p l o t

4.4 *Transferring Letters*

In these questions one letter from the first word is removed and placed in the second word, so that two new words are formed. The letters of the original words always stay in the same order.

Example 1. STORE PLANE

In this example the letter 't' can be removed from the first word to leave the word 'sore'. The 't' can be placed at the end of the second word to make the word 'planet.'

Now try these:

1. CAT HOSE Letter ____ Words ______________ and ______________
2. BREAK TEA Letter ____ Words ______________ and ______________
3. CHOOK AIR Letter ____ Words ______________ and ______________
4. FLOCK AIR Letter ____ Words ______________ and ______________
5. NOTE RIP Letter ____ Words ______________ and ______________

Sometimes more than one letter can be removed from the first word leaving a word. So, if the letter removed from the first word doesn't fit in the second word look to see if there is another letter.

Example 2. TEAR DEER

In this example the letter 'r' can be removed from the first word to leave the word 'tea'. However, we cannot place the 'r' in the second word and get a new word. So we go back to the first word and remove the 't' to leave the word 'ear'. The 't' can be placed between the two 'e's of the second word to make the word 'deter.'

Now try these:

6. METAL PAR — Letter ____ Words ______________ and ______________
7. LOUT MEN — Letter ____ Words ______________ and ______________
8. SPEED SELL — Letter ____ Words ______________ and ______________
9. CHAT CAMP — Letter ____ Words ______________ and ______________
10. LICE SALE — Letter ____ Words ______________ and ______________

4.5 *Practice*

Underline the word that ***can be*** made from the word in capitals.

1. FURTHER - first, tern, rest, hurt, stir
2. REMOVE - money, ever, even, rose, moan
3. POULTRY - role, tool, lout, pole, yours
4. VERBAL - bale, bail, last, ball, belt
5. NATIONAL - tiger, lion, toad, tales, note

Underline one word from each group to make a new word.

6. (if, in it) (at, is, to)
7. (start, stop, begin) (clock, watch, time)
8. (wrist, ankle, foot) (art, print, paint)
9. (son, sun, moon) (face, day, night)
10. (fast, beet, beat) (ten, root, stem)

Complete the third set of words in the same way as the first two sets are made.

11. (mine, miner) (dine, diner) (line,)
12. (last, blast) (lock, block) (leak,)

Complete the second set in the same way as the first set.

13. n e a r [l i n e] s l i d	h e l p [	] b a c k
14. c h a r [f a c e] f u s e	d e a r [	] l i l y
15. v i e w [d o v e] i d o l	s i t e [	] c l a y

Remove a letter from the first word and put it in the second word to make two new words.

16.	FOUR	NIT	Letter ____	Words ________________	and ________________
17.	STONE	TAG	Letter ____	Words ________________	and ________________
18.	FLARE	COD	Letter ____	Words ________________	and ________________
19.	AFAR	RED	Letter ____	Words ________________	and ________________
20.	CHAT	LOUD	Letter ____	Words ________________	and ________________

Chapter 5: Codes

5.1 Simple Substitution Codes

In simple substitution codes, each letter of the word is always coded for by the same letter or number.

In these questions write the word above the code you are given. Then ask the question "Am I going code to word or word to code?" Then put an arrow in that direction. Then work out each letter of the word or code you are given, always working in the direction of the arrow.

Example 1: In a particular code the word FRIENDLY was coded for by the code GHSRTYED. What is the code for the word RIFLE?

Firstly we write the word FRIENDLY above the code.

F R I E N D L Y
G H S R T Y E D

Then ask the question: "Is it word to code or code to word?" Put an arrow in that direction. We are going word to code so I put an arrow in that direction.

↓ F R I E N D L Y
G H S R T Y E D

Now I look at every letter in the word RIFLE and following the direction of the arrow look at what code represents that letter. R is coded for by H, so that is the first letter of our code. We continue with the remaining letters to get HSGER. So HSGER is our answer.

Example 2: In a particular code the word ENCLOSURE was coded for by the code 263845172. What does the code 61752 mean?

Firstly we write the word ENCLOSURE above the code.

↑ E N C L O S U R E

2 6 3 8 4 5 1 7 2

Then ask the question: is it word to code or code to word. Put an arrow in that direction. We are going code to word so I put an arrow in that direction.

Now I look at every digit in the code 61752 and following the direction of the arrow look at what letter is represented by each code. 6 codes for N, so that is the first letter of the word. We continue with the remaining letters to get NURSE. Nurse is a word, so that is the answer.

Now try these:

1. If the code for I N S T E A D is 3 4 5 8 2 1 7, what is the code for I N D E E D? _________

2. If the code for I G N O R E is 5 9 2 3 1 8, what does 1 8 9 5 3 2 mean? _________

3. If the code for T A L E N T is 5 2 3 7 6 5, what is the code for L A T E? _________

4. If the code for G I R A F F E is 3 2 7 8 4 4 1 what is the code for F A R E? _________

5. If the code for R E A D is 2 3 8 5, what does 5 8 2 3 mean? _________

6. If the code for T E N O R is W A S D Y, what does S D W A mean? _________

7. If the code for P E A C H is L O E H B, what is the code for C H E A P? _________

8. If the code for F L E A S is V A S W E, what does A S W V mean? _________

9. If the code for S W O R D is B X A D W, what does W A A D mean? _________

10. If the code for M E S S A G E is S M E E P L M what is the code for G A M E S? _________

5.2 Adding and Subtracting Codes

In these codes the letter is a number of letters up or down from the code. In these questions write the word above the code you are given. Then ask the question "Am I going code to word or word to code?" Then put an arrow in that direction. Then work out each letter of the word or code you are given, always working in the direction of the arrow.

Example 1: In a particular code the word VALVE was coded for by the code WDQCN. What is the code for the word STEAM?

Firstly we write the word VALVE above the code.

V A L V E
W D Q C N

Then ask the question: is it word to code or code to word. Put an arrow in that direction. We are going word to code so I put an arrow in that direction.

↓ V A L V E
W D Q C N

Now I look at every letter in the word VALVE and following the direction of the arrow look at how many forwards or backward in the alphabet the code letter is. V is coded for by W which is forwards one, so I write +1 underneath. Continue with the other letters.

↓ V A L V E
W D Q C N
+1 +3 +5 +7 +9

Whatever, is done for the given word, for the other word do ***exactly the same***.

S T E A M
+1 +3 +5 +7 +9
T W J H V

So the code for STEAM is TWJHV.

Now try these:

1. If the code for N O T E is M N S D, what is the code for B O O K ? __________

2. If the code for W O R K is X N S J, what does Q K B X mean? __________

3. If the code for B L U E is C N V G, what is the code for A Q U A? __________

4. If the code for G R E E N is F P D C M what is the code for B R O W N? __________

5. If the code for W A T E R is U B R F P, what does B S G O I mean? __________

6. If the code for R O L L is Q M I H, what is the code for T U R N? __________

7. If the code for S E N D is T G O F, what is the code for P O S T? __________

8. If the code for H O M E is J M O C, what does F M Q P mean? __________

9. If the code for W O R D is V N Q C, what does C N D R mean? __________

10. If the code for M E A N is O G C P what is the code for N I C E? __________

23 24 25 26 1 2 3 4 5 6 7 8 9 10 11 12 13 14 15 16 17 18 19 20 21 22 23 24 25 26 1 2 3 4
W X Y Z A B C D E F G H I J K L M N O P Q R S T U V W X Y Z A B C D

5.3 Number Codes

These are the same as the addition and subtraction codes in the previous section except that the code is written as the number that the letter occupies in the alphabet. It is easiest if you write the numbers above the alphabet.

Example 1: In a particular code the word F O O D was coded for by the code 7 17 18 8. What does 14 7 4 16 code for?

Firstly we write the word FOOD above the code.

F O O D
7 17 18 8

Then ask the question: is it word to code or code to word. Put an arrow in that direction. We are going code to word so I put an arrow in that direction.

↑ F O O D
7 17 18 8

Now, look at every number in the code 7 17 18 8 and following the direction of the arrow look at how many forwards or backward in the alphabet FOOD is. 7 codes for F which is backward one, so write -1 underneath. Continue with the other letters.

↑ F O O D
7 17 18 8
-1 -2 -3 -4

Whatever, is done for the given code, for the other code do ***exactly the same***.

14 7 4 16
-1 -2 -3 -4
M E A L

So the code 14 7 4 16 means MEAL.

23	24	25	26	1	2	3	4	5	6	7	8	9	10	11	12	13	14	15	16	17	18	19	20	21	22	23	24	25	26	1	2	3	4
W	X	Y	Z	A	B	C	D	E	F	G	H	I	J	K	L	M	N	O	P	Q	R	S	T	U	V	W	X	Y	Z	A	B	C	D

Sometimes a code may have a combination of letters and numbers. If asked to find a code, if the code in the question is a number then the code in the answer is a number and if the code in the question is a letter the code in the question is a letter. Whatever the format in the question, the answer should be ***exactly the same***.

Example 2: In a particular code the word W E N T was coded for by the code V 7 M 5. What is the code for GONE?

Firstly we write the word WENT above the code.

W E N T
V 7 M 5

Then ask the question: is it word to code or code to word. Put an arrow in that direction. We are going word to code so I put an arrow in that direction.

↓ W E N T
V 7 M 5

Now, look at every letter in the word WENT and following the direction of the arrow look at how many forwards or backward in the alphabet the code is. W is coded for by V which is backward one, so write -1 underneath. Continue with the rest of the code.

↓ W E N T
V 7 M 5
-1 +2 -1 +2

Whatever, is done for the given word, for the other word do ***exactly the same***. The first digit of the given code is a letter, so the first digit of the answer is a letter. The second digit of the given code is a number, so the second digit of the answer is a number. Continue with the rest of the code.

G O N E
-1 +2 -1 +2
F 17 M 7

So the word GONE is represented by the code F 17 M 7.

23 24 25 26 1 2 3 4 5 6 7 8 9 10 11 12 13 14 15 16 17 18 19 20 21 22 23 24 25 26 1 2 3 4
W X Y Z A B C D E F G H I J K L M N O P Q R S T U V W X Y Z A B C D

Now try these:

1. If the code for F A S T is 5 26 18 19, what is the code for S L O W? _________

2. If the code for S I N G is 20 11 17 11, what does 21 3 15 15 mean? _________

3. If the code for S N O W is 17 12 13 21, what is the code for R A I N? _________

4. If the code for L E N T is 13 4 15 19 what is the code for G I V E? _________

5. If the code for G R O W is 9 21 17 26, what does 22 18 14 7 mean? _________

6. If the code for S T A R is 21 23 5 23, what does 6 24 23 25 mean? _________

7. If the code for M I L E is 14 12 13 8, what is the code for I N C H? _________

8. If the code for D A T E is 3 4 19 8, what does 19 12 12 8 mean? _________

9. If the code for F I N D is 8 K 16 F, what does 14 Q 21 G mean? _________

10. If the code for S O M E is 18 L 8 X what is the code for M O S T? _________

5.4 *Alphabet Reflections*

In these codes the code is the same distance from the end of the alphabet as the word. They can also be thought of as reflections around the middle of the alphabet. The middle of the alphabet is between the letters M and N. I am going to refer to the point between M and N as the midline.

If in a code question, V codes for E, have a look to see if it is a reflection code. While, many codes have A coding for Z, Y for B or M for N as they are only adding or subtracting one or two, very few codes use add or subtract nine.

Example: In a particular code, the code for M A K E is N Z P V, what is the code for L A W N?

M is one letter to the left of midline and A is one letter to the right; A is the first letter of the alphabet and Z is the last; K is three letters to the left of the midline and P is three letters to the right; E is the fifth letter of the alphabet and V is five letters from the end of the alphabet.

So, for the word LAWN:
L is 2 letters to the left of the midline, so the code will be 2 letters to the right of the midline, which is O.
A is the first letter of the alphabet, so the code will be the last letter of the alphabet, which is Z.
W is the fourth last letter of the alphabet, so the code will be the fourth letter which is D;
N is the letter to the right of the midline, so the code is the letter to the left of the midline which is M.
Therefore, the code for LAWN is OZDM.

23 24 25 26 1 2 3 4 5 6 7 8 9 10 11 12 13 14 15 16 17 18 19 20 21 22 23 24 25 26 1 2 3 4
W X Y Z A B C D E F G H I J K L M N O P Q R S T U V W X Y Z A B C D

Now try these:

1. If the code for N I N E is M R M V, what is the code for S E N D? _________

2. If the code for S A V E is H Z E V, what does D R M W mean? _________

3. If the code for S O R E is H L I V, what is the code for H U R T? _________

4. If the code for W E N T is D V M G what is the code for H I V E? _________

5. If the code for T E S T is G V H G, what does V C Z N mean? _________

6. If the code for R O S E is I L H V, what does U Z O O mean? _________

7. If the code for M I L K is N R O P, what is the code for C A L F? _________

8. If the code for N O T E is M L G V, what does K V M H mean? _________

9. If the code for W HA T is D S Z G, what does G S R H mean? _________

10. If the code for G A M E is T Z N V what is the code for P L A Y? _________

5.5 *Practice*

1. If the code for F I R E is G J S F, what is the code for R A I N? ________

2. If the code for S O R R Y is T Q S T Z, what does U J B P L mean? ________

3. If the code for A W N I N G is Y U L G L E, what is the code for W I N D O W? ________

4. If the code for S H I R T is T J L V Y what is the code for S H O E S? ________

5. If the code for E J E C T I O N is G H G A V G Q L, what does C G T A T Y H R mean?________

6. If the code for W H I T E is Z I L U H, what does V I D S N mean? ________

7. If the code for R U B B E R is X Z F E G S, what is the code for C O T T O N? ________

8. If the code for G R A D E is 6 17 26 3 4, what does 5 8 17 18 19 mean? ________

9. If the code for F A M I L Y is 7 26 14 8 13 24, what does 7 17 10 4 15 3 mean? ________

10. If the code for S T U N T is Q R S L R what is the code for M O V I E? ________

23	24	25	26	1	2	3	4	5	6	7	8	9	10	11	12	13	14	15	16	17	18	19	20	21	22	23	24	25	26	1	2	3	4
W	X	Y	Z	A	B	C	D	E	F	G	H	I	J	K	L	M	N	O	P	Q	R	S	T	U	V	W	X	Y	Z	A	B	C	D

11. If the code for M O U S E is 19 20 25 22 7, what is the code for T W I R L? _________

12. If the code for S A F A R I is 20 25 7 25 19 7, what does 16 19 21 4 10 18 mean? _________

13. If the code for J U N G L E is 11 W 15 I 13 G , what is the code for F O R E S T? _________

14. If the code for H O R S E is 9 Q 21 W 10 what 19 K 7 I 23 mean? _________

15. If the code for S C O P E is Q 1 M 14 C, what the code for W I D T H? _________

16. If the code for Z E B R A is A V Y I Z, what does T I Z H H mean? _________

17. If the code for C I R C L E is, X R I X O V what is the code for S Q U A R E? _________

18. If the code for S E N S E is H V M H V, what does G Z H G V mean? _________

19. If the code for H E A D is S V Z W, what does G Z R O mean? _________

20. If the code for S U P E R is H F K V I what is the code for G R E A T? _________

Chapter 6: Mathematical VR

6.1 Links

In this type of question the numbers in the third group must be connected in the same way as the first two groups. Find out how the middle number relates to the two outside numbers for the first groups and then do exactly the same for the third group.

Example 1: 5 (7) 2   3 (8) 5   1 ( ) 9

In the first group 5+2=7, so we add the outside numbers to get the middle number. We check this with the second group and 3 + 5 = 8. In the third group we do exactly the same, add the two outside numbers and 1 + 9 = 10. So our answer is 10.

If the number in the middle is bigger than the outside numbers we must use addition or multiplication. If it goes up a little it is probably addition and if it goes up a lot it is probably multiplication. If the number in the middle is smaller than either of the outside numbers we must use subtraction or division. If it goes down a little it is probably subtraction and if it goes down a lot it is probably division.

Now try these:

1.	6 (8) 2	7 (10) 3	1 ( ) 5
2.	10 (2) 5	20 (5) 4	14 ( ) 7
3.	9 (5) 4	7 (4) 3	4 ( ) 1
4.	1 (3) 2	2 (4) 2	3 ( ) 2
5.	2 (10) 20	4 (10) 40	7 ( ) 70
6.	3 (7) 4	2 (8) 6	3 ( ) 2
7.	2 (6) 3	5 (5) 1	3 ( ) 5
8.	1 (8) 9	2 (7) 9	4 ( ) 6

9. 8 (7) 1 6 (4) 2 5 ( ) 3

10. 3 (30) 10 3 (12) 4 2 ( ) 2

Sometimes there are two steps to get the middle number.

Example 2: 3 (10) 2 4 (14) 3 1 ( ) 3

Answer: There are two possibilities for 3 (10) 2.

Firstly, you could multiply (3 x 2 = 6) then add four (6 + 4 = 10).

Then, test with the second group: 4 x 3 = 12, then 12 + 4 = 16.

This doesn't work, so you need to find another possibility.

You could add (3 + 2 = 5) then multiply by two (5 x 2 = 10).

Then test with the second group: 4 + 3 = 7, then 7 x 2 = 14.

This works, so to the third group we do exactly the same: add the two outside numbers then multiply by two. 3 equals four, times two equals 8 (1 + 3 = 4, then 4 x 2 = 8).

So our answer is 8.

Now try these:

11. 2 (5) 2 3 (9) 5 7 ( ) 3

12. 4 (40) 5 3 (12) 2 5 ( ) 2

13. 3 (31) 10 9 (91) 10 7 ( ) 10

14. 4 (8) 2 6 (11) 3 5 ( ) 2

15. 5 (15) 2 4 (20) 4 6 ( ) 5

16. 5 (7) 4 4 (8) 6 12 ( ) 4

17. 4 (6) 3 10 (11) 2 6 ( ) 5

18. 3 (12) 8 5 (10) 4 10 ( ) 6

19. 8 (7) 1 6 (8) 4 5 ( ) 3

20. 9 (33) 11 6 (8) 4 6 ( ) 5

6.2 Mathematical Substitution

In these questions you need to replace the letters with the numbers given in the question. The maths symbols stay the same. Then you do the maths problem. If it asks you for the answer as a letter you then need to convert the answer to the letter.

Example 1: A=1, B=3, C=2

A + C = _____ Give the answer as a letter

First we substitute the letters for the numbers and write them underneath and so we get

A + C = _____ Give the answer as a letter
1 + 2 =

Then we complete the maths and 1+2=3. If the question asked for the answer as a number the answer would be 3. As it asks for the answer as a letter we look back to the top of the question. B=3, so our answer is 'B'.

Now try these:

Give the answer as a ***number***.

1. A = 1, B = 3, C = 4

   A + B = _____

2. B = 2 C = 5 E = 4

   B x C = _____

3. A = 2 B = 3 C = 8

   C ÷ A = _____

4. A = 11, B = 10, C = 6

   B - C = _____

5. A = 3, B = 4, C = 5

   A + C = _____

Give the answer as a ***letter***.

6. A = 2, B = 3, C = 4, D = 5

   A + B = _____

7. A = 2, B = 3, C = 6, E = 7

   A x B = _____

8. A = 2, B = 3, C = 4, D = 8

   C ÷ A = _____

9. A = 2, B = 3, C = 4, D = 8

   D - C = _____

10. A = 1, B = 2, C = 3, D= 6, E = 7

    B x C + A = _____

6.3 *Equalities*

In these questions whatever the left of the equals sign is worth, the right must be worth exactly the same. To do these work out what one side equals and make the other side the same.

Example 1: 11 + 39 = 30 ÷ 3 x ____

Firstly, calculate the left hand side. 11 + 39 = 50. Since the left hand side equals fifty, the right hand side must also equal fifty. The right hand side, 30 ÷ 3 = 10. Therefore, 10 x the answer must equal fifty. To work this out we can do the opposite of multiplication which is division. 50 ÷ 10 = 5, so our answer is 5.

Example 2: 32 x 4 = 16 x ___

When both sides is only multiplication, often you do not need to work out what each side equals. This is the only exception. As 16 is half of 32, the second number must be double. Double 4 is 8. The reason this works is that it doesn't matter which order multiplication is done in. Therefore (16 x 2) x 4 = 16 x (2 x 4).

Now try these:

1. 12 + 6 = 20 - ___
2. 20 x 3 = 50 + ___
3. 11 x 2 – 2 = 5 x ___
4. 14 ÷ 2 + 4 = 2 x 2 + ___
5. 5 x 3 = 2 x 10 - ___
6. 17 - 8 = 81 ÷ ___
7. 23 – 2 = 7 x ___
8. 99 ÷ 9 = 88 ÷ ___
9. 6 x 4 +4 = 15 x 2 - ___
10. 5 + 6 + 4 + 2 = 30 – 3 – 6 - ___

6.4 *Number Sequences*

To continue a sequence you need to work out the pattern. The pattern can involve addition, subtraction, multiplication or division. Always write down your working out.

Example 1: 2 5 11 23 ___

In this example when we look at the difference between numbers.

$2\ ^{+3}\ 5\ ^{+6}\ 11\ ^{+12}\ 23$ ___

Each time we are doubling what we add. So for the next number we will add 12 x 2, which is 24. 23 add 24 is 47, so the answer is 47

Example 2: 20 18 15 13 10 8 ___

In this example when we look at the difference between numbers

$20\ ^{-2}\ 18\ ^{-3}\ 15\ ^{-2}\ 13\ ^{-3}\ 10\ ^{-2}\ 8$ ___

In this example, we are subtracting 2, 3, 2, 3, 2, so next we will subtract 3. 8 – 3 is 5, so the answer is 5.

Now try these:

1.	3	5	7	9	11	___
2.	27	24	20	17	13	___
3.	1	2	4	8	16	___
4.	3	6	10	15	21	___
5.	500	450	400	350	300	___

Sometimes, the pattern is a "skipping" or "leapfrogging" pattern. In these patterns, every second number makes a pattern. If it is this type of pattern, then the remaining numbers will also make a pattern.

Example 3: 2 20 4 23 6 26 8 ___

In this example if we look at every second number we get:

+2 +2 +2

2 20 **4** 23 **6** 26 **8** ___

The numbers go forward by two each time. Looking at the numbers in-between these numbers:

+3 +3 +3

2 **20** 4 **23** 6 **26** 8 ___

The numbers go forward by three each time. So three will be added to the 26, giving the answer of 29.

Now try these:

6. 2 10 5 7 8 ___
7. 20 14 18 12 16 ___
8. 80 8 70 7 60 6 50 ___
9. 1 4 2 8 3 12 4 ___
10. 20 12 17 9 14 ___

6.5 *Practice*

Work out how the first two sets of numbers are connected and work out the number in the middle of the third set.

1. 12 (15) 3 27 (32) 5 16 ( ) 8
2. 20 (5) 4 18 (3) 6 27 ( ) 9
3. 5 (12) 2 3 (14) 4 2 ( ) 9
4. 41 (20) 2 34 (3) 11 17 ( ) 4
5. 21 (50) 4 34 (88) 10 12 ( ) 3

Give the answer to the following questions as a letter.

6. A = 7, B = 6, C = 13, D = 15

   A + B = _____

7. A = 9, B = 7, C = 60, D = 63, E = 3

   A x B - C= _____

8. A = 2, B = 3, C = 4, D = 8, E = 1 6

   D ÷ A = _____

9. A = 2, B = 4, C = 8, D = 12, E = 22

   D - C - A = _____

10. A = 20, B = 5, C = 3, D= 10, E = 15

    B x C - B = _____

Work out the missing number.

11. $34 \times 27 = \_\_\_\_ \times 34$

12. $56 - 6 = 45 + \_\_\_\_$

13. $22 \div 2 = 11 \times \_\_\_\_$

14. $13 + 6 = 23 - \_\_\_\_$

15. $12 \times 2 + 6 = 5 \times \_\_\_\_$

Work out the next number in these sequences.

16. 3 6 12 24 ____

17. 27 24 21 18 ____

18. 9 13 17 21 ____

19. 2 5 7 10 ____

20. 4 22 6 20 ____

Chapter 7: Puzzling VR

7.1 Mixed-up Codes

In these questions, there are a number of words and codes, but they are mixed up. There is normally either one more code than word, or one more word than code. This means you must make sure that there is only one possibility, before deciding a particular number codes for a particular letter. To work these out, work out what one letter codes for, because of a double letter, or because the letter is in the same place in more than one word. Then place that letter above each of that number. Continue until you work out all the words. Then, work out the questions using the deciphered code.

Example:

SAND	SING	LONE	LINE
2 6 5 7	2 9 5 7	4 6 5 8	

What does 5 6 5 7 mean?

In this example, that there are two numbers starting with a 2, does not help as there are two words starting with an 'S' and two starting with an 'L.' There are two numbers ending with a '7' and 'E' is the only letter which ends two or more words, so '7' must be 'E.' Above all the 'E's write the number '7'. There are two words where the second letter is I and two numbers with the second letter '6'. So above all the 'I's, I write '6'. My words now look like this:

	6	7	6 7
S A N D	S I N G	L O N E	L I N E

I can now see that the word 'line' is coded for by a number 'something', 6, 'something', 7. This must be 2 6 5 7, So I write 2, 6, 5, 7 above LINE. This means L must be 2, so I write '2' above all the 'L's and 'N' must be 5, so I write '5' above all the 'N's. LONE is now 2, 'something, 5, 7 so must be 2 9 5 7. SING is now 4, 6, 5, 'something.
So must be 4 6 5 8.
My words now look like this:

4 5	4658	29 57	2657
SAND	SING	LONE	LINE

Now I can use the codes I have worked out to work out what 5 6 5 7 means. 5 means 'N', so I can write N above both 5s. 6 means I, so the second letter is I. 7 means E so my last letter is E. Therefore 5 6 5 7 codes for N I N E.

Now try these:

Three of the four words are given in code. The codes are not written in the same order as the words and one code is missing.

FARM PERM RATE LAST

4163 5342 7142

1. Find the code for the word M A T E. ____________
2. Find the word that has the code 7 3 1 4. ____________
3. Find the code for the word T A P E. ____________

Three of the four words are given in code. The codes are not written in the same order as the words and one code is missing.

LACE SENT NOTE TEEN

1573 3557 7635

4. Find the code for the word N E S T. ____________
5. Find the word that has the code 3 5 7 3. ____________
6. Find the code for the word T O N E S. ____________

Three of the four words are given in code. The codes are not written in the same order as the words and one code is missing.

SAFE	FAST	GROW	BEAR
4 2 7 5	6 7 3 1	3 7 6 2	

7. Find the code for the word S T A R. ____________________
8. Find the word that has the code 6 7 5 2. ____________________
9. Find the word that has the code 5 7 1 3. ____________________
10. Find the code for the word B E S T. ____________________

7.2 *Go with Two Groups*

In this type of question you need to work out which word goes with both groups of words. These questions tend to use words that have more than one meaning. Try each word in turn and see if it goes with both pairs.

Example: (glue, paste) (branch, twig) adhesive, cut, stick, tree, kindling

Look at the first word 'adhesive'. Ask if it goes with the first set of words. It does so, go to the second set. It doesn't go with the second set. So go to the next word 'cut'. Ask if it goes with the first set of words. It doesn't so, go to the next word, 'stick.' Ask if it goes with the first set of words. It does so, go to the second set. It also goes with the second set, so the word 'stick' is the answer.

Now try these:

Underline the word that goes equally well with both pairs of words.

1.	(rod, cane) (employees, workers)	staff, company, boss, stick, stake
2.	(second, day) (large, tiny)	hour, minute, week, big, small
3.	(flower, daisy) (up, incline)	tulip, rose, orchid, dandelion, hill
4.	(arrive, disembark) (ground, earth)	soil, land, sand, depart, stop
5.	(gram, ounce) (rock, boulder)	kilogram, pebble, gem, stone, mineral
6.	(dog, rabbit) (freckle, pimple)	cat, mole, giraffe, lizard, wart
7.	(near, far) (shut, open)	away, here, push, pull, close
8.	(pence, dollar) (gram, stone)	cent, pound, yen, ounce, kilogram
9.	(novel, magazine) (order, reserve)	book, journal, newspaper, request, buy
10.	(level, horizontal) (house, bungalow)	straight, apartment, vertical, residence, flat

7.3 Word Analogies

In this type of question, there must be the ***same connection*** between each set of words. So if the first set are opposites, then the second set must also be opposites.

That is, the way the second word is made is exactly the same for each pair. So whatever you do for the first pair, to the second you do ***exactly the same***.

Example: June is to (March, July, month) as Tuesday is to (week, Monday, Wednesday)

June is to month is related as June is a month BUT Tuesday is a day and 'day' is not an option. June is related to July, as July comes immediately after June. Wednesday comes immediately after Tuesday, so Wednesday is the answer.

Now try these:

1. First is to (third, second, aqua) as gold is to (grey, green, silver)
2. Stale is to (fresh, hard, mouldy) as clean is to (polluted, old, tidy)
3. Horse is to (pony, foal, donkey) as fox is to (calf, cub, kitten)
4. Wine is to (drink, whine, meal) as dear is to (expensive, deer, cheap)
5. Lion is to (cub, pride, savannah) as fish is to (scales, swim, school)
6. Left is to (write, right, correct) as yes is to (no, not, maybe)
7. Cheese is to (cow, milk, biscuits) as books are to (information, novel, paper)
8. Speak is to (shout, talk, whisper) as business is to (account, firm, hard)
9. Butcher is to (meat, meet, shop) as bakery is to (scones, ovens, bread)
10. Hammer is to (tool, nail, wood) as stapler is to (punch, staple, join)

7.4 Belonging to a Group

In this type of question, there are a number of words that have something in common, You must decide which of the other words given, go with this group of words.

Example: Underline the word in brackets which goes with this group of words:

lemon, orange, grapefruit (strawberry, lime, banana)

Answer: lemon, orange and grapefruit are all citrus fruit. Lime is a citrus fruit, so that is the answer.

Example 2: Underline the word in brackets which goes with this group of words:

been, floor, sheet (tart, bean, little)

Answer: been, floor and sheet all have a double letter. Little has double 't', so little is the answer.

Now try these:

Underline the word in brackets which goes with this group of words:

1. first, last, gold (second, race, yellow)
2. heart, kidneys, brain (legs, body, lungs)
3. London, Paris, Vienna (Greece, Athens, Germany)
4. butcher, supermarket, bakery (shop, meat, newsagent)
5. baby, toddler, adult (teenager, young, puberty)
6. teacher, nurse, secretary (electrician, build, bake)
7. car, train, bus (taxi, plane, boat)
8. knife, wriggle, when (went, whole, winter)
9. willow, oak, hazel (acorn, ash, bark)
10. whiteboard, desk, chair (teacher, projector, fridge)

7.5 Practice

Three of the four words are given in code. The codes are not written in the same order as the words and one code is missing.

W R E N   W I S E   L I T E   S O R E

2 3 7 4   2 1 4 8   5 3 9 4

1. Find the code for the word T I L E. __________________
2. Find the meaning of 7 9 4 2 __________________
3. Find the meaning of 2 3 8 8 4 1 __________________

Three of the four words are given in code. The codes are not written in the same order as the words and one code is missing.

B O A T   T H A T   F O R E   R I T E

6 7 3 4   1 9 4 5   4 2 3 4

4. Find the code for the word T O T E. __________________
5. Find the meaning of 2 5 3 1 4 2 __________________
6. Find the code for the word H E A T __________________

Underline the word that goes equally well with both pairs of words.

7. (look, check) (ring, necklace) anklet, bracelet, watch, pendant, broach
8. (tiger, monkey) (hold, carry) cat, gorilla, lion, bear, giraffe
9. (finger, hand) (screw, hammer) nail, wrist, knuckle, screwdriver, chisel
10. (gone, departed) (right, up) remain, leave, down, diagonal, left

Underline a word from each set of brackets to complete the sentences below.

11. Drink is to (thirst, water, drank) as find is to (found, look, lose).
12. Ewe is to (sheep, ram, flock) as doe is to (dog, stag, boar).
13. Find is to (lose, found, locate) as construct is to (misplace, demolish, pretend).
14. Snow is to (wind, rain, flakes) as rain is to (sky, drops, wet).
15. Pane is to (window, pain, glass) as weigh is to (pound, scale, way).

Underline the word in brackets which goes with this group of words:

16. Bowl, plate, mug (cup, spoon, serve)
17. Ten, twenty, fifty (three, twelve, hundred)
18. Violin, cello, viola (flute, oboe, double bass)
19. Pentagon, octagon, decagon (square, cube, sphere)
20. Courgette, sweetcorn, pea (been, bean, apple)

Chapter 8: Logical Word Problems

8.1 What Number?

In these questions an age or a quantity needs to be worked out. To do these questions, start with the number that is given in the question and write the number above the names as they are worked out.

Example: Alfie, Beatrice, Chloe, David and Edward receive their pocket money on a Friday. Alfie was given twice as much as Chloe, who was given £5 more than David. Beatrice was given £2 less than Chloe. Edward didn't receive any pocket money as he has been naughty that week. Beatrice received £6.
How much did David receive?

We start with Beatrice, as we are given how much she received in the question. So we write £6 above Beatrice on the first line. We know that Beatrice received £2 less than Chloe, so Chloe must have received £8. So we write £8 above Chloe on the first line of the question. Alfie received twice as much as Chloe, so he must have received £16. David received £5 less than Chloe so must have received £3. Edward received £0. Now with all the amounts written above the names in the first line, we can simply look and see that £3 is written above David, so our answer in £3.

Now try these:

1. Luke and Ruth are brother and sister. Luke is half Ruth's age, who is a quarter of their Mum's age. If Luke is six years old next year how old is their Mum? ______

2. Archie, Brian, Clive, Deborah and Elise sent texts to their friends on their mobile phones. Archie sent 5 more texts than Brian, who sent two more texts than Clive. Deborah sent 2 less texts than Elise. Clive sent twice as many texts as Deborah. Elise sent 7 texts. How many texts did Archie send? ______

3. Friends Patricia, Joanna, Larena, Alison and Diya enjoy going to the theatre. Over the holidays Patricia goes to the most shows, attending two more than Joanna. Larena goes to more shows than Joanna but less than Patricia. Alison went to two more than Diya who went to two less than Joanna. Diya went to one show. Which two friends went to the same number of shows? ________________ and ________________

4. Sophia, Abigail, Ethan and Jayden collect stamps. Sophia has three times as many as Abigail. Ethan has one hundred more than Abigail but two hundred and fifty more than Jayden. Jayden has only recently started collecting and has fifty stamps. How many stamps does Sophia have in her collection? ______

5. Arran, Botan, Chin, Gan and Huan sat a maths exam. There was a total of thirty marks. Arran gained five marks more than Botan. Chin scored the same as Botan which was ten marks more than Gan. Huan scored full marks, and five marks more than Arran. What was Gan's mark? ______

6. Gunneet, Baljeet, Jacqui and Isabella were counting up their money. Gunneet had three 10p pieces and four 2p pieces. Baljeet had two 20p pieces and four 5p pieces. Jacqui had twelve 2p pieces and Isabella had two 20p pieces and eight 2p pieces. Who had the most money? ______________

7. A zoo had lots of big cats including lions, tigers, cheetahs and panthers. The zoo had two more lions than it had panthers. There were more tigers than panthers but less tigers than lions. There zoo had two cheetahs, one less than the number of panthers. How many lions did the zoo have? ______

8. Nicole, Quinlan, Jenny, Sophie and Hasnain go into a gift shop. Nicole bought two more gifts than Quinlan who bought six more gifts than Jenny, Sophie bought four gifts which was two more than Hasnain. Hasnain bought one more gift than Jenny. How many gifts did Quinlan buy? ______

9. A group of friends made a tally of the number of vehicles travelling past their scout hall. There were fifty more cars than any other type of vehicle. There were two trucks. There were three more buses than trucks and twenty more motorbikes than buses. How many vehicles passed the scout hall altogether. ______

10. Xu-Min, Richard, Oliver and Sonja go to a conference. Xu-Min makes 5 more pages of notes than anyone else. Sonja makes four pages of notes. Oliver makes six less pages of notes than Xu-Min and less pages than Sonja. Richard takes no notes as he has a photographic memory. How many pages of notes did Oliver make? ______

8.2 What Time?

These questions constitute a range of problem solving questions involving time. Generally, these questions can be answered either by breaking the question up into individual steps or by drawing a table. Always start with the information that you know.

The answer should be in the same format as the question. If the question is in 12 hour format don't forget the a.m. /p.m. If the question is in 24 hour format then the answer should be too.

Example 1: Fiona takes 12 minutes to walk to the train station. She needs to catch the 10:15 am train. Her watch is 5 minutes fast. What time does she need to leave, according to her watch?

Answer: This type of question is done in two steps. Start with the time you know (10:15 a.m.). It takes her 12 minutes to walk from the station so subtract 12 minutes from 10:15 a.m.. This gives 10:03 a.m.. Then her watch is 5 minutes fast, so add five minutes on to 10:03 a.m. which gives 10:08 a.m. This can also be done diagrammatically, as shown on the right.

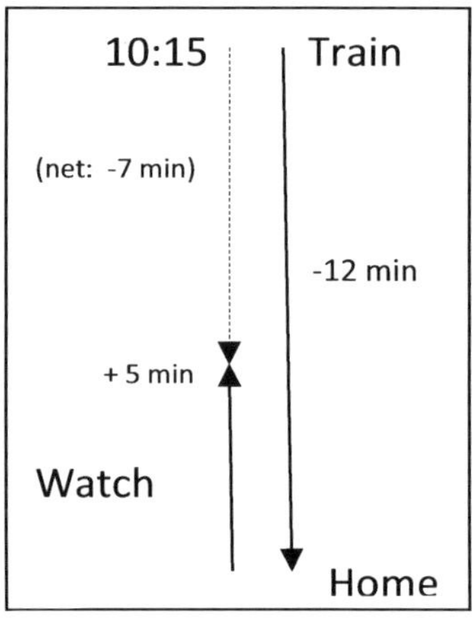

Another type of time question is best done by drawing a table.

Example 2: At an airport three planes depart during the day for Three Springs. Plane A departs at 08:00 and arrives at 12:00. Plane B departs two hours after plane A. Plane C departs three hours after plane B and arrives at 16:00. Plane B takes an hour longer than Plane C. At what time does Plane B arrive in Three Springs?

Answer: Fill data from question into table. The data that is calculated from the other information given is in brackets.

Plane	Depart	Arrive	Flight duration
A	08:00	12:00	(3)
B	(10:00)		Plane C + 1 (4)
C	(13:00)	16:00	(3)

So Plane B must arrive 4 hours after 10:00, which is 14:00. So the answer is 14:00.

Now try these:

1. Paul is three months older than Susan and five months younger than William. Jill was born six months before Peter who was born on the same day as Susan, in September. In what month was the oldest person born? ___________

2. Zheng needs to catch the 8:10 a.m. train to work. He has a 7 minute walk to the station. His watch is 6 minutes fast. What time does he need to leave for the station according to his watch? ______

3. Annice and Alira are going on holiday. They need to be at the airport by 10:30p.m.. The airport is a 35 minute drive away. If their kitchen clock is twenty minutes fast, what is the time the kitchen clock will show, when they need to leave home? ______

4. George wanted to ring Elizabeth who was living in Australia. The time where Elizabeth is living is 9 hours in front of the UK. George rang Elizabeth at 4:00p.m. his time and Elizabeth was not happy. What was the local time when Elizabeth answered the phone? ______

5. Lisa was cooking a roast for dinner. The instruction says that the roast takes 20 minutes for every 500g plus 30 minutes. How long will the roast take if it weighs 1.25 kg? ______

6. A group of friends; Torina, Helen, David, Sian, Sarah and Connor all had their eighteenth birthdays coming up. Helen was the oldest and eight months older than the youngest. David was only a month younger than Helen and born the month before Sian. Sian was born three months before Connor. Sarah was born a month before Connor, who was born in September. In what month was Torina born? ____________

7. Buses stop at Main Street every twenty minutes. It takes thirty minutes to travel by bus to the next town, Townville. If Francis just misses a bus, how long will it be before he gets to Townville? _______

8. Three planes leave from Heathrow for Santina each day. Plane A leaves at 09:00 and arrives in Santina at 14:00. Plane B leaves two hours after Plane A and takes an hour longer than Plane C. Plane C arrives in Santina at 18:00 having departed at 12:00. What time does plane B arrive in Santina. _______

9. In 1807 slavery was abolished in the UK. William Wilberforce, who was born in 1759, started campaigning 20 years before the bill was passed. How old was Wilberforce when he started campaigning to end the slave trade in England? _______

10. The union between England and Wales, began in 1284 with the Statute of Rhuddlan. Much later, in 1707, England and Scotland agreed to join as Great Britain. Nearly a century later, in 1801, Ireland joined the union and became the United Kingdom of Great Britain and Ireland. In 1921, with the Anglo-Irish treaty, Southern Ireland became independent; six northern Irish counties remained part of the United Kingdom as Northern Ireland and the current name of the country, the United Kingdom of Great Britain and Northern Ireland, was adopted in 1927. How long was the South of Ireland part of Great Britain? _______

8.3 Can or cannot be true

In these questions a number of statements are written. You need to decide according to the information whether the statements can or cannot be true. Go through each statement in turn to determine if it is true or not.

You must read the question and determine if you are looking for the statement that must, can or cannot be true. In these questions look out for the keywords: always, every, sometimes, never and often.

Example: Four friends; Agnetha, Benny, Bjorn and Anni-Frid wrote some songs. Benny wrote the most songs. Agnetha wrote more than Anni-Frid. Bjorn wrote more than Anni-Frid. Which statement ***cannot*** be true?

A. Bjorn and Agnetha wrote the same number of songs.

B. Benny wrote the most songs

C. Benny and Bjorn wrote the same number of songs

D. Anni-Frid wrote the least songs.

Answer: First read the question. The question asks for the statement that cannot be true. Then, go through the statements in order, eliminating them in turn.

A. Bjorn wrote more than Anni-Frid and less than Benny, as did Agnetha. So that *could* be true.

B. Benny wrote the most songs, as we are told that. So that is true.

C. Benny wrote the most songs, so must have written more songs than Bjorn. So that cannot be true.

D. As Benny wrote the most songs and both Agnetha and Bjorn wrote more songs than Anni-Frid, this must be true.

As C cannot be true, C is our answer.

Now try these:

1. Three friends; Jerome, Wycliffe and Tyndale each knew several languages. Some of the languages they spoke are now mentioned. Wycliffe and Tyndale both spoke English while Jerome spoke Greek and Latin. Tyndale spoke both Greek and Hebrew. Which statement cannot be true?
    A. Wycliffe only spoke English
    B. Tyndale spoke the most languages
    C. Jerome lived in the fourth century
    D. Wycliffe was the only person who didn't speak Greek.

2. Asif, Brett, Charlotte, Doug and Eric did a Maths test. There were ten questions.
   Asif got full marks.
   Brett left out three questions.
   Charlotte and Doug got the same mark.
   Eric got the second lowest mark, with two more marks than the lowest person.
   Which statement cannot be true?
    A. Brett got the lowest mark.
    B. Doug got the lowest mark.
    C. Brett got six out of ten.
    D. Asif got double Charlotte's mark.

3. Ignacy, Elsie, Treasure, Gordon and Violet did a Maths test. There were ten questions.
   No half marks were awarded.
   Ignacy made no errors.
   Elsie left out three questions.
   Treasure and Gordon got the same mark.
   Violet got half Elsie's mark.
   Which statement can be true?
    A. Elsie got 7 out of 10.
    B. Gordon scored higher than Treasure.
    C. Violet scored 4 out of 10.
    D. Elsie scored 6 out of 10.

4. Mario, Luigi, Peach and Bowser are exploring the Solar System. Mario always follows Peach to the planet she is on. Luigi visits the rocky planets: Mercury, Venus, Earth and Mars. His brother, Mario visits the gaseous planets Jupiter and Saturn. Peach has now moved to Uranus. Mario encountered Bowser on Jupiter and Peach encountered him on Uranus. Bowser is currently on Neptune. Which of the following must be true?
   A. Luigi and Peach have visited the same number of planets.
   B. Mario will go to Uranus next
   C. Bowser throws fire at Mario
   D. Luigi doesn't like gas planets

5. Liam, Geoff, Dayan and Tom participate in the sack race at a charity sports event.
   The winner didn't fall.
   Tom was last.
   Dayan passed Liam.
   Only Geoff fell.
   Which of the following statements must be true?
   A. Dayan and Geoff finished at the same time.
   B. Geoff withdrew injured.
   C. Liam came second.
   D. Dayan won the sack race.

6. Danielle, Caitlin, Lara and Alisha played a handball round robin. Each student played every other student. Danielle, Caitlin and Lara drew games. Alisha won all of her games. Which statement cannot be true?
   A. There were three drawn games.
   B. Lara won all her games.
   C. Caitlin drew two games.
   D. Six games were played.

7. Bill, Hazel, Marina and Toyen speak at a conference. Marina, who was the only person who spoke after lunch, spoke the longest. Bill and Hazel gave a joint presentation that lasted for five minutes less than Marina spoke for. Toyen only spoke for ten minutes before lunch but had an informative question session afterwards. Which of the following statements cannot be true?
   - A. There were three talks altogether.
   - B. Toyen was the second last speaker.
   - C. Bill and Hazel spoke last.
   - D. Marina spoke for 20 minutes.

8. Satvir, Corinne, Xanthe and Yvonne played Tennis. In the first round Satvir played Corinne and Xanthe played Yvonne, the winners going through to the next round. Xanthe beat Corinne three games to two. Which of the following cannot be true?
   - A. Xanthe lost no games.
   - B. Corinne lost half of the games she played.
   - C. Satvir lost all of her games.
   - D. Xanthe lost more games than Satvir.

9. Lailla, Melisha, Eisa and Anushka collect coins. Lailla has three times as many coins as Melisha. Eisa has five less coins than Melisha. Anushka has fifty coins. Anushka has less coins than Lailla but more than Melisha.
   Which of the following can be true?
   - A. Lailla has 65 coins.
   - B. Lailla has 42 coins.
   - C. Eisa has 52 coins.
   - D. Lailla has 57 coins.

10. Meg, Jo, Beth and Amy knitted squares to make a blanket. Beth who is ill knitted the most squares, including all the ones that went around the outside of the blanket. Meg and Amy knitted the same number of squares. Jo knitted no squares, but would sit by Beth's bed and sew the squares together. Which of the following statements must be true?

    A. Meg and Amy spent the same time on the blanket.
    B. Beth knitted twice as many squares as Meg.
    C. Jo knitted the least number of squares.
    D. Meg knitted more squares than Amy or Jo.

8.4 Sorting Information

In these questions, the information in the question needs to be sorted, in some way for the answer to be determined.

The simplest type of these questions is where all that is needed is to work out how many each person has. For this type, simply write how many above each name.

Example 1: Isla, Mia, Mileet and Savi have pets. Isla, Mia and Mileet each have a fish. Mileet and Savi have a guinea pig each. Isla and Mileet have a dog. Mia has a horse and a rabbit. Who has the least pets.

Answer: Go through each person in turn counting how many pets each person has. Isla has a fish and a dog. So write '2' above Isla's name. Mia has a fish, a horse and a rabbit, so write '3' above Mia's name. Mileet has a fish, a guinea pig and a dog so write '3' above Mileet's name. Savi has a guinea pig so write '1' above Savi's name. Savi is the only child with only one pet, so Savi is the answer.

In some questions, counting is not sufficient to determine the answer. Sometimes, the information can be arranged into a table. However, it can be quicker to just work through the information in the question rather than drawing a table, ruling out possibilities at each step.

The table is only used to answer the question and is not marked. As in the 11+ you will generally have an average of about 40 seconds per question, the table needs to be drawn quickly with as many abbreviations as possible.

Example 2: Paramjit, Anne, Millie, Jacqui and Christine go to the zoo. Paramjit, Anne and Millie buy their lunch there while Jacqui and Christine bring a packed lunch. Anne, Millie and Jacqui love the gibbons while Paramjit and Christine prefer the meerkats. Jacqui and Christine bring an umbrella while the others bring a raincoat. Everyone except Millie wear boots. Millie wears trainers. Anne and Paramjit wear a scarf.

Who likes Meerkats and brought an umbrella?

Answer (Method One): Reading through the question look for who likes meerkats. This narrows the possibilities to Paramjit and Christine. Then look for who bought an umbrella. Out of Paramjit and Christine and Christine bought an umbrella. So Christine is our answer.

Answer (Method Two): Put the information in the question into a table, abbreviating everything. Abbreviate the names to their first letter.

	Lunch	Ani	Rain	Scarf
P	Buy	Meer	r-c	
A	Buy	Gib	r-c	✓
M	Buy	Gib	r-c	
J	Pac	Gib	Umb	✓
C	Pac	Meer	Umb	

Once the table is drawn, look down the animal column for meerkat. First we find ‘P’. Look across and under rain is raincoat so it is not ‘P.’ Continue looking down animals. Christine likes meerkats and when you look across you will see that Christine also has an umbrella. So the answer is Christine.

Now try these:

1. Ryan, Lacey, Nasir and Vera play musical instruments. They all learn the recorder at school. They also have the option of learning a brass instrument during school and Ryan and Lacey do this. Lacey, Nasir and Vera all have the same piano teacher, who also teaches Vera the violin. Ryan and Nasir both learn the flute but only Nasir is learning the piccolo. Who is learning the most instruments?

2. Felicity, Gaynor, Hamza and Isidore were discussing the activities they do after school. Hamza and Isidore have piano lessons after school, while Felicity has violin lessons. Gaynor and Hamza are both part of the local scout group. Felicity and Isidore both go to the youth group at the local church. Hamza loves his horse-riding on a Tuesday night. Isidore and Gaynor play badminton every Thursday. Isidore does not like football, while Hamza enjoys playing it weekly. Who does the most after-school activities?

3. Ryan, Vipul, Jorge and Kane are in the same swimming club, which meets Saturdays and Tuesday evenings at six o'clock. Last week Ryan and Vipul swam 100 laps. Jorge swam 60 while Kane swam 20. Vipul is never late for swimming but Jorge is often late. Kane is sometimes late but arrived early last week. Vipul was the slowest, while Kane was the fastest. They all finished at 7:00p.m.. When they weren't swimming they didn't stay in the water. Who spent the most time out of the water last week?

4. Aleeyah, Kiera, Nalina and Ashley play a game involving throwing a dice. Aleeyah is the only one who threw a six. Kiera and Nalina threw the same number. Ashley threw two less than Nalina. Aleeyah, Kiera and Ashley all threw different numbers. Which of the following can be true?
   A. Ashley threw a four.
   B. Kiera got three more than Nalina.
   C. Kiera threw a two.
   D. Nalina threw a four.

5. Three friends: Mansi, Natalie and Ola go clothes shopping. Mansi and Natalie both buy a new top. Ola really likes the skirt and top outfit she bought as well as her new dress. Mansi bought some new school shoes while Ola bought some nice court shoes to go with her new dress. Who bought the most articles of clothing?

6. Thakshna, Anita, Kamwar and Ursula sit the 11+ exam. Thakshna and Anita are hoping for the same school and need a score of 111 to get in. Kamwar is going for a boys' grammar school and this year the cut off was 132. Ursula needs 126 to get into her school of choice. They all score 123. Which of the following must be true?
   A. They all get into their school of choice.
   B. None of them get a place at a grammar school.
   C. Thakshna and Anita are the only ones to get in to the school of their choice.
   D. Kamwar is the only one not to get a place in a grammar school.

7. A, B, C, D and E are books.
   A and B are reference books.
   C and D are novels.
   E is a biography.
   D and E are paperbacks, while the rest are hardback.
   A, C, D are children's books while the rest are for adults.
   Which book is a children's non-fiction book?

8. Five friends: Amelia, Ryszard, Cytanna, Niamh and Pierre go shopping for a mobile phone. All except Amelia want a phone that plays music. Ryszard, Cytanna and Niamh want a smart phone with internet access. All but Pierre want a camera on their phone to take photos. Amelia and Ryszard also want a phone to take short videos. Who wants a phone that plays music, has internet access and takes videos?

9. Townville, Little Chalet, Villagette, Seasiding and Beach Estate are seaside holiday resorts. Townville, Little Chalet and Villagette have caravan parks on the beach, the others do not have a caravan park. They all have fish and chip shops. Little Chalet, Seasiding and Beach Estate have amusement parks. Townville and Seasiding have a show at their showgrounds in summer. Beach Estate and Townville have surfing lessons. Beach estate is the only one with dolphin watching.
   Which resort would you recommend for someone who needs a caravan park and wants to visit a show but does not want the noise of an amusement park?

10. Joelle, Rolf, Haidee, Dalton and Willow are very active. Joelle enjoys running, cycling, swimming, hockey and badminton. Rolf swims and cycles. Haidee plays netball, hockey and badminton. Dalton, plays not only all the sports that Joelle plays but also plays volleyball. Willow plays netball, hockey and volleyball. How many people cycle?

8.5 Practice

Use the information below to answer questions one to five.

Priyanka, Rakesh, Simon, Terrence, Moira and Winston are learning languages at University.

They all speak more than one language.

Priyanka speaks Hindi, English and French.

Rakesh speaks Hindi and English.

Simon speaks English, French and German, Spanish and Portuguese.

Terrence speaks English, German and Cantonese.

Moira speaks Russian, Portuguese, French, Spanish and English.

Winston speaks Punjabi, Mandarin, Japanese and English.

1. If the above is correct, which of the following must be true?
   A. They all want to be translators.
   B. None of them speak Polish.
   C. The university is in England.
   D. Simon is the most fluent in French.

2. Apart from English what is the most common language spoken? ______________

3. Who speaks German but not French? ______________

4. Amongst each other, if they were not allowed to speak English who could speak to the most people? ______________

5. If they were not allowed to speak English who would not be able to communicate orally with anyone? ______________

6. Five friends: Benedict, Courtenay, Edwin, Fahima and Gerald measure their height. Benedict is taller than Courtenay but not as tall as Edwin. Courtenay is shorter than Edwin but taller than Fahima. Fahima is taller than Gerald but shorter than Courtenay. Which of the following statements must be true?
   A. Courtenay is the second tallest.
   B. Edwin is the shortest.
   C. Edwin has finished growing.
   D. Gerald is the shortest.

7. Five children: Hilda, Ida, Julian, Katrina and Lawrence are 15, 13, 12, 12 and 10 years old. Two of the children are twins. Hilda is one year older than Ida. Katrina is two years younger than Julian. Lawrence is three years older than Julian. Which two children are twins?__________ and __________

Look at the following train timetable to answer questions 8 and 9. Assume all trains travel at the same speed.

	Train A	Train B	Train C	Train D
Fenchurch	14:17	14:42	15:17	15:42
Green Village	14:23	14:48	15:23	15:48
Small Town	14:41	15:06	15:41	16:06
Middlemarch	15:02	15:27	16:02	16:27

8. Joy has to be in Small Town by 4:00p.m.. If she just misses the train, how many minutes late will she be? __________

9. Sue works in Middlemarch. It takes her 15 minutes to walk from Middlemarch station to work. When she is on the afternoon shift she has to be at work by 4:00p.m.. Which train does she need to catch from Fenchurch?

____

10. There is a row of five houses. Sean lives beside Edgar. Sean also lives next door to Roslyn. Edgar lives next to Kim and Roslyn lives next to Pascal. They all live in separate houses. Which of the following must be true.

    A. Sean lives next door to Pascal.

    B. Kim lives next to Roslyn.

    C. Edgar lives next to Roslyn.

    D. Sean is in the middle.

Chapter 9: English VR

9.1 Comprehension

Reading comprehension refers to the understanding and analysis of written English passages. While the simplest questions involve a simple understanding of the words and finding the answer in the passage; more difficult questions require analysis and interpretation.

Example: Read the excerpt below from "The World I Live in" by Helen Keller.

My hand is to me what your hearing and sight together are to you. In large measure we travel the same highways, read the same books, speak the same language, yet our experiences are different. All my comings and goings turn on the hand as on a pivot. It is the hand that binds me to the world of men and women. The hand is my feeler with which I reach through isolation and darkness and seize every pleasure, every activity that my fingers encounter. With the dropping of a little word from another's hand into mine, a slight flutter of the fingers, began the intelligence, the joy, the fullness of my life.

1. With what part of her body does Helen Keller access the world?
    A. Eyes
    B. Ears
    C. Hands
    D. Feet

2. In this passage what does Helen Keller mean when she writes that we travel on the same highways?
    A. She drives on the same streets and roads as her readers
    B. Her experiences are the same as ours
    C. We share the same way of life
    D. We wear the same shoes

3. What type of writing is this?
   A. Novel
   B. Biography
   C. Encyclopaedia entry
   D. Textbook

In the first question, we are asked what part of the body Helen Keller uses to access the world. The passage clearly informs the reader that Helen Keller accesses the world through the hand; particularly in the first sentence when the passage states that "My hand is to me what your hearing and sight together are to you." So the first answer is her hands.

In question 2 of the example, we are asked what it means that "we travel on the same highways." This is asking you to recognise metaphorical (figurative) language. As this phrase is not literal, it cannot be answers A or D. Her experience is different to us, as in the second sentence it says "yet our experiences are different". However, the passage says that the world we live is the same and she is accessing the same world with her hands. So the answer to the second question is that "We share the same way of life."

In question 3 of the example, we are asked for the type of writing. As it is about some-one (Helen Keller) it is a biography (We can refer to it more specifically as an autobiography as the author, Helen Keller, is talking about herself. An autobiography is a type of biography).

So the answers will look like this:

1. With what part of her body does Helen Keller access the world?
   A. Eyes
   B. Ears
   C. <u>Hands</u>
   D. Feet

2. In this passage what does Helen Keller mean when she writes that we travel on the same highways?
   A. She drives on the same streets and roads as her readers
   B. Her experiences are the same as ours
   C. <u>We share the same way of life</u>
   D. We wear the same shoes

3. What type of writing is this?
   A. Novel
   B. Biography
   C. Encyclopaedia entry
   D. Textbook

Read the following passage:

Plastics made from crude oil are just over a hundred years old. Plastic means pliable and easily shaped. That plastics are lightweight and strong and able to be easily moulded makes them incredibly useful. Over the last century plastics have become ubiquitous and are found in every area of our lives.

Plastics were initially hailed as a huge asset for both people and the environment. Plastics which were originally created as an alternative to ivory. Plastic was seen as saving elephants and tortoises. It appeared that plastics could protect the natural world from destruction by humans for required materials.

However, it was not long that another side of plastics was seen and concern grew that the effect on the environment was not so positive. That plastics do not break down meant that a bottle of water that may take ten minutes to drink could remain in landfill for thousands of years.

Since plastics are now viewed to be essential to modern life in computers, mobile phones and medicinal applicators, some scientists are working to develop plastics that are safer and more sustainable. For example, they are developing plastics that biodegradable.

1. According to the passage, which of the following is not a benefit of using plastic?
   A. Flexible.
   B. Light.
   C. Long lasting.
   D. Strong.

2. What is meant be the term ubiquitous?
   A. All the time.
   B. Everywhere.
   C. Important.
   D. Cheap.

3. How were plastics initially seen.
   A. Entirely positive.
   B. Entirely negative.
   C. Neutral.
   D. Both positive and negative characteristics.

4. Which word best describes the author's view of plastics in the world today.
   A. Useful but problematic.
   B. Useful and necessary.
   C. Pollution problem that requires a ban on their use.
   D. Ornamental.

5. Where might you find the above?
   a. A novel
   b. A handbook
   c. A zoo newsletter
   d. An atlas

Read the following passage from Aesop's Fables, "The Fox and the Crow."

> A Fox once saw a Crow fly off with a piece of cheese in its beak and settle on a branch of a tree.
>
> "That's for me, as I am a Fox," said Master Reynard, and he walked up to the foot of the tree.
>
> "Good-day, Mistress Crow," he cried. "How well you are looking to-day: how glossy your feathers; how bright your eye. I feel sure your voice must surpass that of other birds, just as your figure does; let me hear but one song from you that I may greet you as the Queen of Birds."
>
> The Crow lifted up her head and began to caw her best, but the moment she opened her mouth the piece of cheese fell to the ground, only to be snapped up by Master Fox.

"That will do," said he. "That was all I wanted. In exchange for your cheese I will give you a piece of advice for the future. Do not trust flatterers"

6. Who is the narrator?
   a. The fox.
   b. The crow.
   c. The cheese.
   d. A third person narrator.

7. What does the moral, "Don't trust flatterers," mean?
   a. Only trust people that compliment you.
   b. Don't trust people that flatter you because it means they're jealous of you.
   c. Just because someone flatters you doesn't mean they truly care about you.
   d. Watch what people do rather than just what they say.

8. According to the passage what does caw mean?
    a. A beautiful song.
    b. A beak.
    c. To cry.
    d. To speak in melodic tones.

9. Which word best describes the fox?
    a. Angry.
    b. Devious.
    c. Candid.
    d. Friendly.

10. What is the lesson of the story?
    a. People should share food with friends, or they may lose it all.
    b. Think about what you are going to do before you act.
    c. Tricky people will be punished in the end.
    d. Be careful who you talk to.

9.2 Cloze

These questions are sentences with words missing. The correct word must be chosen from a choice of words in order to make a sensible, grammatically correct sentence.

The following need to be considered:

- Tense (past, present or future)
- Singular and plural
- General grammar
- Vocabulary – the meaning of the words.

After you have chosen the words, read your answer back to yourself, and check that the sentence makes sense.

Example: My brother and (me, myself, I) went to the zoo (tomorrow, yesterday, sometime) and (he, she, you) liked the tigers best.

Answer: The first word must be I, as the grammar must be correct, the second word must be yesterday as the verb 'went' is in the past tense. The third word must be he as it refers to 'my brother' who is male.

So the complete sentence is: My brother and ***I*** went to the zoo ***yesterday*** and ***he*** liked the tigers best.

Now try these:

1. The (builder, teacher, doctor) taught the (patient, house, student) (how, when, where) to do long division.
2. The Earth (orbits, rotates, climbs) the (sun, moon, stars) once a (day, month, year).
3. The acorn is the (seed, leaf, book) (of, have, about) the (beech, willow, oak) tree.
4. Every Friday, she (went, goes, go) shopping, but next Friday (is, was, were) Good Friday, so the shop will be (closed, close, opening).
5. The farmer (give, sells, buys) the (blood, meat, milk) from his (pigs, goats, horses) to the cheese factory.
6. Brenda was very excited to (love, become, get) a grandmother (of, for, at) the (beginning, first, once) time.
7. The boy is very (disappointed, excited, scared) that (there, her, his) birthday is in three (day, years, weeks) time.
8. Many species of animals (is, are, will) endangered and could (be, become, are) extinct if we do (no, not, be) care for them.
9. The (oldest, historic, capital) city of (Ireland, Wales, Scotland) is (Edinburgh, Paris, London).
10. There was an (pile-up, accident, collision) on the motorway (yesterday, tomorrow, London), which caused a traffic (marmalade, honey, jam).

9.3 Two Words In Between

In this type of question, there are two words. You need to put two words in the middle so that only one letter changes each time.

Example 1: S O A P

_____

_____

F L A N

Firstly, notice which letter is already the same. This must stay the same. So 'A' will remain. Then change any of the other letters to that of the final word. In our example if we change the 'O' to an 'L' we get 'SLAP.' Now it is the same as the questions you did in "middle words" earlier in the book. Now 'L' and 'A' are the same as the final word. So these must stay the same. If we change the 'S' to an 'F ' we get 'FLAT.' Now, the last letter, 'P' can be changed to 'N' make our final word, FLAN.

S O A P
S **L** A P
F L A P
F L A **N**

Notice only one letter changes each time.

Now try these:

1. C A S E

   ______

   ______

   F O R E

2. L A C E

   ______

   ______

   F A S T

3. R E N T

   ______

   ______

   B E A N

4. L A S T

   ______

   ______

   L O N E

5. S P O T

   ______

   ______

   P L O P

6. S L A P

   ______

   ______

   F L O W

7. N O S E

   ______

   ______

   R O L L

8. T H A T

   ______

   ______

   C O A L

9. S A F E

   ______

   ______

   B A L D

10. G R A N T

    ____

    ____

    B L A N D

9.4 Extra Word?

In these questions there are the words of a sentence jumbled up with one or more extra words. Determine what the sentence is, then find the word that remains.

Example: flat battery start end car wouldn't because the the was

The sentence is: The car wouldn't start because the battery was flat.

So the missing word left over is 'end'.

Now try these:

1. the every Olympic dream Games years are four held
2. is to eat it drink important diet healthy a
3. the equator is north south and hemispheres divides the
4. reads wrote plays poems William Shakespeare lots of and
5. are primitive native kangaroos Australia to animals
6. was used reeds to make paper first were the
7. bread wheat ground flour is the into to make
8. star our in solar system stars sun the is the
9. to vocabulary a books reading an helps good build
10. brush will healthy teeth keep to them your should you

9.5 Practice

Read the passage below from Jane Eyre by Charlotte Bronte.

This room was chill, because it seldom had a fire; it was silent, because remote from the nursery and kitchen; solemn, because it was known to be so seldom entered. The house-maid alone came here on Saturdays, to wipe from the mirrors and the furniture a week's quiet dust: and Mrs. Reed herself, at far intervals, visited it to review the contents of a certain secret drawer in the wardrobe, where were stored divers parchments, her jewel-casket, and a miniature of her deceased husband; and in those last words lies the secret of the red-room—the spell which kept it so lonely in spite of its grandeur.

1. From the above passage only, the room was
   A. Small and unusable
   B. Large and bare
   C. Haunted
   D. Large and impressive

2. Why does Mrs Reed visit the room
   A. To view the contents of her secret drawer
   B. To make sure the maid does her job
   C. To speak with her husband
   D. To dust the room

3. Who visits the room most often?
   A. Mrs Reed
   B. The maid
   C. Mrs Reed's husband
   D. Jane Eyre

4. What mood does the narrator create about the red room?
    A. Warm and friendly
    B. Cold and foreboding
    C. Derelict
    D. Cosy

5. Why is the room so little used.
    A. They don't want to damage the furniture.
    B. It's too dirty and will being in there will get their clothes filthy.
    C. It's too far from the rest of the house.
    D. It holds too much grief for her.

In these questions, choose the correct word in each set of brackets to make a sensible, grammatically correct sentence.

6. The (builder, plumber, electrician) (plumb, wired, electric) the house before it could be (fenced, sold, built).
7. A rhombus has (four, six, twelve) equal (sides, angles, corners) but (no, none, some) right angles.
8. Plants use (carbon dioxide, oxygen, nitrogen) from the air to make glucose (and, but, also) release (carbon dioxide, oxygen, nitrogen).
9. Nocturnal (plants, animals, cows) are (active, asleep, wake) during the (night, midday, midnight).
10. (Friction, magnetism, electricity) is a (force, push, static) that (opposes, helps, grows) motion.

In these questions change the first word one letter at a time to make the final word. Each step must be a correctly spelt word.

11. S T O P

    ______

    ______

    S H I N

12. F A L L

    ______

    ______

    S I L T

13. A M O N G

    ____

    ____

    C L O N E

14. S C O R E

    ____

    ____

    C H O K E

15. S T E M

    ______

    ______

    S H O P

In these questions, a sentence has been jumbled up. One extra word has been included. Write the extra word on the line provided.

16. treats you like would treat others as treated to be ______________

17. four advent Christmas weeks are the before is called ______________

18. lots animals endangered become every year many ______________

19. Easter every changes date moon of the year ______________

20. Mountainous Nepal China India small is a country low between and ______________

Chapter 10: Vocabulary VR

10.1 Crossword Grids

In these questions a number of words are given, which must be placed in the crossword grid.

The clue to this type of question is to ensure that there is only one possible word for a position before putting it in the grid.

Example: Put the words VALUE, PETIT, DAFT, VEST, TRUST, TIRED into the crossword grid below.

V	A	L	U	E

The word going down from the ‘V’ of VALUE must be VEST because it is the only four letter word starting with ‘V’. This means that the word going across the middle must be a five letter word starting with ‘T’. however, there are two possibilities – TIRED or TRUST. However, there is only one four letter word left. So if the four letter word, DAFT, is put in, then the rest of these words follow.

The completed crossword can be seen below:

V	A	L	U	E
E				
S		T		
T	I	R	E	D
		U		A
		S		F
P	E	T	I	T

Now try these:

1. Put these words into the grid below: Short, Start, Abode, Tread, Typed

S	H	O	R	T
	■	■	■	
	■	■	■	

2. Put these words into the grid below: Frown, Tough, Feast, Adopt, Notch

F	R	O	W	N
	■	■	■	
	■	■	■	

3. Put these words into the grid below: Torch, Urban, Truth, Hurry, Honey

T	O	R	C	H
	■	■	■	
	■	■	■	

4. Put these words into the grid below: Shore, Yeast, Exert, Stray, Rinse

S	H	O	R	E
	■	■	■	
	■	■	■	

5. Put these words into the grid below: Train, Taken, Extra, Crest, Chant

				T
	■	■	■	R
				A
	■	■	■	I
				N

6. Put these words into the grid below: Clove, Noses, Oasis, Cabin, Edges

C	L	O	V	E
	■		■	
	■		■	
	■		■	

7. Put these words into the grid below: Ethos, Every, Dew, Sorts, Elder, Yawns

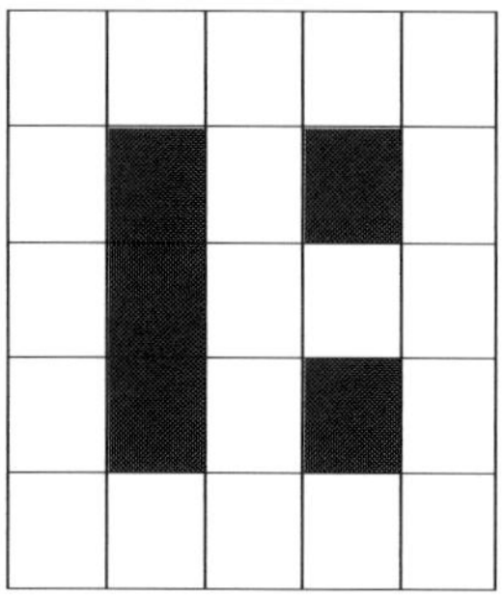

8. Put these words into the grid below: Ate, Toe, Tee, Now, Ewe, Ant

A	T	E

9. Put these words into the grid below, so that each word appears twice in the grid:
Acre, Haul, Leek, Urge

A	C	R	E

10. Put these words into the grid below: Tower, Least, Lakes, Spear, Eh, Sow, Ahi, Aisle

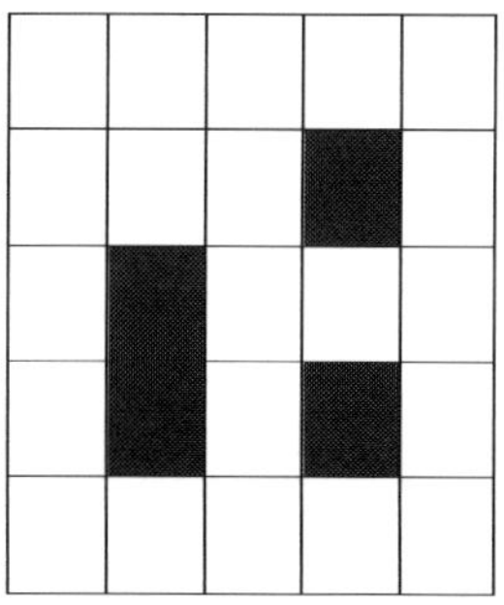

10.2 Crossword Clues and Definitions

These questions involve finding the word that fits the definition and any letters given.

Example 1: Complete the word below that matches the word given.

S	T			U	

3D artwork.

Answer: A statue is a piece of 3D artwork. So the word statue is completed in the boxes.

S	T	A	T	U	E

3D artwork.

Now try these:

1.

D					I		N

Money or goods given to charity

2.

	H			B		

A polygon with four equal sides

3.

L				B		

Able to be read

4.

G			T				D	

Thankfulness

5.

	O	C		

Adjust to get a clear image

Sometimes, you may be asked for the word, the word which rhymes with another word or the word which fits in alphabetical order.

Example 2: Write the word which rhymes with the word in capitals, and has the meaning given in the clue.

COW Part of a tree

Answer: a BOUGH is part of a tree and rhymes with cow. So bough is the answer.

Example 3: Write the word which would come between the given words in a dictionary and has the meaning given.

SALUTE

_______ Wild, not tame

SWING

Answer: SAVAGE means wild and comes between salute and swing in a dictionary. So savage is the answer.

Now try these:

Write the word that rhymes with the word in capitals and has the meaning given.

6. BLACK loose ___________
7. BALL messy handwriting ___________

Write the word which would come between the given words in a dictionary and has the meaning given.

8. end

   ________________ a short journey carrying a message

   error

9. eject

   ________________ intricate and rich in detail

   elect

10. cure

   ________________ the flow of electricity in a circuit

   curse

10.3 Letters Missing

In a sentence, one word is missing a number of letters. These do not necessarily make a word.

Example: An encyclopaedia is a REFCE book.

The full word should be REFERENCE

We already have the letters REFCE:

REF<u>EREN</u>CE
REF   CE

So the answer is EREN.

Now try these:

1. They were PED and ready for the trip.
2. She always went SWIMG on Monday.
3. WEDAY is the third day of the working week.
4. She PRACTD the piano every day.

<u>Soap</u>

5-10 The origins of soap making are unknown. The first CON□□□TE evidence of soap making comes from Ancient Babylon and dates back to around 2800 B.C. They mixed boiling ashes together with animal and VEG□□□BLE fats to make a slurry that they used for cleaning. The next recorded making of soap was from Egyptian papyri, around 1500 BC. The Egyptians mixed fats with alkaline salts. By 200 AD the Romans were using soap in their baths.

The IN□□□TRIAL revolution bought new MET□□□S of making soap. Exotic fragrances were □□□ORTED from Africa and Asia, making soap more AP□□□LING.

10.4 Scrabble Words

In these questions a long word is given and a number of words need to be found, that can be made from the letters of the long word, using each letter only once, and have the meaning given.

To do this, think of the letters of the long word as being scrabble tiles, which can then be moved around to make other words.

Example: Using the letters of the word EQUILATERAL make words that mean:

1. The same: _______________
2. Attached to the back of an animal: _______________

EQUAL means the same and can be made from the letters of EQUILATERAL.

TAIL is something that is attached to the back of an animal and can be made from the letters of EQUILATERAL.

So the answer to one is EQUAL and two is TAIL.

Now try these:

Using the letters of the word TRIANGLE make words that mean:

1. A female child _______________
2. A metal _______________
3. Jewellery worn on the finger _______________
4. How old someone is _______________
5. A strong wind _______________

Using the letters of the word DIVISIBLE make words that mean

6. To say something that is not true ______________
7. Remain alive ______________
8. Past tense of to bleed ______________
9. To enter a swimming pool ______________
10. Move smoothly ______________

10.5 Practice

1. Put these words into the grid below: Sea, Ada, Era, Had, She, Ear

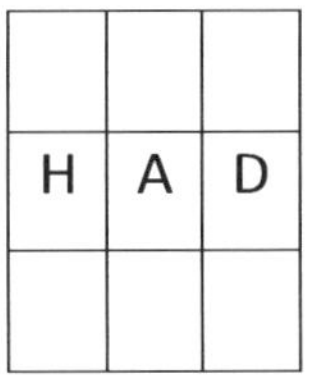

2. Put these words into the grid below: Fiver, Safer, Solid, Dared, Rapid

3. Put these words into the grid below: Email, Excel, Stone, Sea, Basic, Sabre

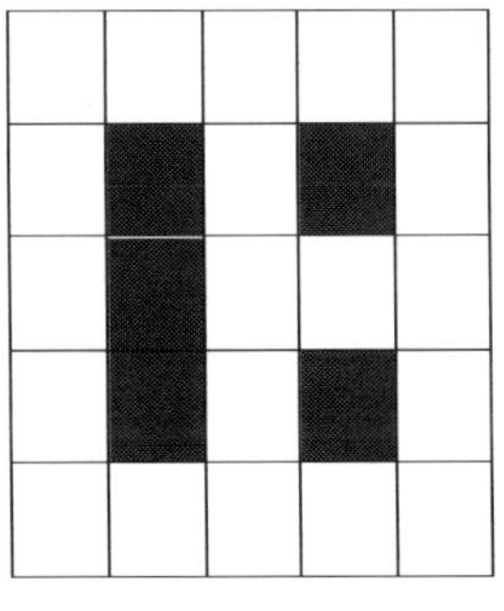

4. Put these words into the grid below: Genus, Germs, Relay, Lea, Scale, Style

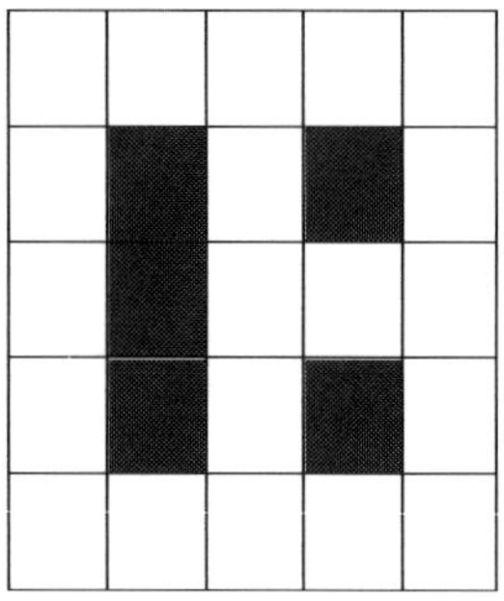

5. Put these words into the grid below, so that each word appears twice in the grid:

   Acetic, Pierce, Regret, Spread, Errata, Detach

A	C	E	T	I	C

Complete the following definitions.

6.

W			

Document stating what will happen to a person's property after they die.

7.

			L			y

Series of three books.

8.

T			N			

A large tidal wave caused by an earthquake or volcano.

9.

H	O				T		B		E

Friendly and welcoming to visitors and guests.

10.

	R		V	

To be courageous.

Write the letters missing from the word in capitals.

11. Seonaid enjoyed going SING for her Mum's birthday present. ______

12. PRACT makes perfect. ______

13. The temperature was extremely hot in the Sahara DRT. ______

14. They used a map to work out DIRIONS. ______

15. The wedding was a very special OCION. ______

Using the letters of the word SCIENTIFIC make words that mean the following:

16. A smell ______________

17. A number ______________

18. Tightly stretched, taut ______________

19. A pleasant sunny day ______________

20. Instructed to go to a particular destination. ______________

Chapter 11: Even More Words

11.1 Two Letters Between

In these questions, two letters are needed to finish the first word and start the second. These are much harder than questions missing one letter as you cannot simply go through the alphabet from A to Z. When there are two pairs of words, the same two letters must be used for both pairs.

To answer these questions find as many two letter combinations that will finish the first word and see if these letters complete the other words. If you run out of letters you can think of for the first word, try completing one of the other words.

Example: E A ( ) A R T L A ( ) R I N G

Answer: 'CH' would make the first word EACH and the second word CHART. However, in the second set of words LACH is not a word. 'ST' makes the words EAST, START, LAST and STRING, so the answer is 'ST.'

Now try these:

1.	FREE( )BRA	GRA( )AL
2.	SHO( )AL	BEHA( )ST
3.	GROW( )REE	BA( )IRST
4.	FIR( )REET	LI( )RONG
5.	WHI( )ETH	HAS( )RM
6.	YELL( )NER	FOLL( )LS
7.	BRID( )AR	LAR( )RMS
8.	CL( )AZE	STE( )USE
9.	FRI( )IT	BLE( )GE
10.	EX( )EM	FRU( )CH

11.2 Anagrams

In these questions, the letters of a word have been jumbled up. Using the clue or the context of the sentence unjumble the letters.

It may help to rewrite the letters in a different order or in an irregular pattern.

Example 1: PECLIN Can be used to write with.

Answer: Pencil – You can write with a pencil.

Example 2: A rose is a TRANRAGF flower.

Answer: A rose is a FRAGRANT flower.

Now try these:

In these questions rearrange the word in capitals so that the sentence makes sense.

1. The boy typed his story on the PUTCOMRE. ______________
2. You must be IESTNL during a test. ______________
3. There were lots of PHEELNATS at the zoo. ______________
4. The doctor PCRREBDSIE antibiotics for the bacterial infection. ______________
5. The builder used MEILTNOES to build the wall. ______________
6. The class VRAAEEG for the test was seven out of ten. ______________

In these questions rearrange the word in capitals to make a word that means the following.

7. CCRSUI Where clowns perform. ______________
8. YURNCET A hundred years ______________
9. JFYSTIU Explain to prove something is right or reasonable. ______________
10. ORRTMOWO The next day ______________

11.3 Word in Front

In these questions, you need to find a single word that when placed in front of all of the given words, makes a valid compound word.

Example: guard, time, line, boat

Answer: If the word 'life' is placed in front of each word it makes the compound words: lifeguard, lifetime, lifeline and lifeboat. So the answer is 'life.'

Now try these:

1. due, turn, take, all ________________
2. ward, tune, go, bid ________________
3. do, grow, live, wards ________________
4. rise, light, burn, day ________________
5. bone, chat, date, drop ________________
6. age, ball, step, note ________________
7. age, port, word, able ________________
8. arm, man, cracker, work ________________
9. light, line, rest, ache ________________
10. bank, paper, castle, pit ________________

11.4 Word Structure

These questions look at the letters within a word or the sound of the word. There are three types:

i. Which words have the same letters?

ii. Which words are palindromes?

iii. Rhyming words.

Example 1: Underline the two words below that consist of the same letters.

claim could loud cloud maced

Answer: could and cloud both contain the letters c,d,l,o,u. So the answer is could and cloud.

Example 2: Underline the word which is a palindrome (spelt the same forwards and backwards)

stop peanut tops radar repair

Answer: radar is the same read forwards and backwards. So the answer is radar.

Example 3: Underline the two words which rhyme.

bough low cow fluff cliff

Answer: bough and cow both have the same sound at the end of the word. So the answer is bough and cow.

Now try these:

Underline the two words made of the same letters.

1.	rugged	ought	drugged	graded	tough
2.	chart	flats	start	tarts	torch
3.	thin	sheep	peach	hint	chear

Find an anagram (a word containing the same letters) for the following:

4. owlet ________________

5. forts ________________

6. swaps ________________

Underline the word below which is a palindrome.

7.	canoe	yacht	kayak	swallows	follow
8.	music	strut	minim	clef	trust

Underline the two words below that rhyme.

9.	rough	growth	berth	truth	stuff
10.	cheque	break	brick	wreck	quit

11.5 Practice

In these questions write the two letters in the brackets that finish the first word and start the second. It must be the same two letters for both pairs of words in each question.

1. B E A (   ) A R T   T O R (   ) E S S

2. F O R (   ) L L   G R A (   ) N T R E

3. F U T U (   ) A L I S E   S T O (   ) A C H

4. F R E (   ) O R T   S P L A (   ) O U T

5. O C E (   ) Y O N E   S W (   ) N O Y

In these questions rearrange the word in capitals, so that the sentence makes sense.

6. You must put your SHRUBBI in the bin.

7. The dark grey LUCODS suggested a storm was likely.

8. The flautist played in the local CHERRTOAS.

9. You should always STENIL and obey your parents.

10. The art shop had a large TMASSORENT of coloured pencils.

Find a word that can go in front of each word to make a compound word. Put that word in the space provided.

11. front lift root set ___________

12. ball cover ware wood ___________

13. bag out rail writing ___________

14. gull side shore weed ___________

15. age card code pone ___________

Underline the two words that are made of the same letters.

16. front easel lease trees stirs

17. night attic tactic thing want

18. board flesh half drab shelf

19. street shrub trees brush bush

Underline the word below that is a palindrome.

20. tacit grown wrong racecar remember

Some Useful Vocabulary Lists

Common English trees
Ash
Beech
Birch
Elm
Hazel
Larch
Maple
Oak
Pine
Poplar
Willow
Yew

Common English Flowers
Bluebell
Buttercup
Carnation
Cornflower
Daisy
Daffodil
Dandelion
Fuchsia
Geranium
Honeysuckle
Hyacinth
Iris
Rose
Orchid
Pansy
Primrose
Snowdrop
Violet
Wisteria

Common English Birds
Albatross
Coot
Cuckoo
Dove
Duck
Eagle
Finch
Goose
Gull
Heron
Jay
Kingfisher
Lapwing
Lark
Magpie
Moorhen
Owl
Petrel
Plover
Puffin
Quail
Raven
Robin
Rook
Sparrow
Starling
Swallow
Tern
Tit
Wagtail
Warbler
Woodpecker
Wren

Birds of Prey
Eagle
Falcon
Hawk
Kestrel
Owl

Polygons
3 – triangle
4 – quadrilateral
5 – pentagon
6 – hexagon
7 - heptagon
8 - octagon
9 – nonagon
10 - decagon

String instruments
Violin
Viola
Cello
Double bass
Guitar
Banjo
Lute

Brass Instruments
Cornet
Trumpet
Tuba
Trombone
French horn
Bugle

Woodwind instruments
Oboe
Clarinet
Flute
Piccolo
Saxophone
Bassoon

Animal Words

Animal	*Male*	*Female*	*Baby*	*Group*
Antelope	Buck	Doe	Calf	Herd
Chicken	Cock / Rooster	Hen	Chicken	Flock
Cat	Tomcat	Queen	Kitten	
Cattle	Bull	Cow	Calf	Herd
Deer	Buck / Stag	Doe	Fawn	Herd
Dog	Dog	Bitch	Puppy	Pack
Dolphin	Bull	Cow	Pup	Pod
Elephant	Bull	Cow	Calf	Herd / Parade
Fish				School / Shoal
Fox	Tod / Dog/ Fox	Vixen	Cub / Kit / Pup	Skulk / Leash
Giraffe	Bull	Doe	Calf	Herd / Corpse / Tower / Group
Goat	Billy	Nanny	Kid	
Horse	Stallion	Mare	Foal	Herd / Stable
Lion	Lion	Lioness	Cub	Pride
Pig	Boar	Sow	Piglet	
Rabbit	Buck	Doe	Kitten	
Sheep	Ram	Ewe	Lamb	Flock
Squirrel	Buck	Doe	Pup / Kitten	Dray
Zebra	Stallion	Mare	Colt / Foal	Herd / Crossing

Answers

1.1 Letter Sequences

1. R,U
2. N, R
3. A, Y
4. N, I
5. A, C
6. N, P
7. O, N
8. E, D
9. P, T
10. A, Z

11. G, G
12. BV, EX
13. EL, FN
14. MP, PS
15. HR, LP
16. EF, FG
17. IJ, KL
18. TS, RQ
19. UJ, ZQ
20. WS, RV

1.2 Analogies

1. PQ
2. TU
3. FD
4. HL
5. SR
6. DG
7. BX
8. YA
9. IJ
10. GF

1.3 Order of size

1. 3
2. thirteen
3. 3:00 p.m.
4. warm
5. year 1
6. small
7. bad
8. tens
9. London
10. mouse

1.4 Alphabet letters

1. F
2. Y
3. A
4. I
5. N
6. E
7. IT
8. IN
9. T
10. MN (either order)

1.5 Practice

1. KB, LZ
2. MQ, LS
3. NC, PB
4. KH, PF
5. GQ, MS
6. OP
7. KI
8. NR
9. XW
10. TW
11. sentence
12. six
13. third
14. March
15. day
16. H
17. V
18. O
19. O
20. S

2.1 Finish and Start

1. N
2. R
3. M
4. L
5. Y
6. G
7. F
8. T
9. D
10. F

2.2 Alphabetic Order

1. nectarine
2. dictionary
3. orange
4. juice
5. gift
6. plum
7. glass
8. pilot
9. line
10. oregano

2.3 Missing letters

1. SEE
2. TAG
3. SAW
4. TEN
5. RIB
6. HOP
7. AIR
8. HER
9. ACT
10. VAN

2.4 Hidden Words

1. need (cone, edge)
2. shin (hush, in)
3. till (until, later)
4. ship (checks, hippopotasmuses)
5. them (truth, emerged)
6. lick (colic, kept)
7. dear (idea, required)
8. race (another ace)
9. wasp (was, polite)
10. chin (stitch, in)

2.5 Practice

1. T
2. K
3. R
4. Y
5. H
6. lawyer
7. muffins
8. maths
9. money
10. goat
11. PUT
12. HAM
13. AGE
14. LET
15. EAT
16. chin (reach, into)
17. kind (look, India)
18. sent (bass, entered)
19. went (show, entrant)
20. near (deadline, arrived)

3.1 Odd Two Out

1. rainbow, colour
2. clothes, hands
3. rice, pasta
4. ball, racquet
5. house, kitchen
6. reading, writing
7. hen, duck
8. hospital, patient
9. telephone, electricity
10. bread, toast

3.2 Synonyms

1. giggle
2. ill
3. pleased
4. freezing
5. magnify
6. intelligent, clever
7. chair, seat
8. glasses, tumblers
9. add, sum
10. make, create
11. bear
12. scamp
13. assume
14. frail
15. clear
16. kind, type
17. buoyant, cheerful
18. illicit, forbidden
19. glimpse, glance
20. fine, well

3.3 Antonyms

1. all
2. correct
3. white
4. down
5. outside
6. present, past
7. right, left
8. talk, listen
9. few, many
10. food, drink
11. prolong
12. demolish
13. flourish
14. opening
15. fresh
16. cluster, isolate
17. wash, soil
18. attempt, ignore
19. jam, clear
20. maroon, rescue

3.4 Middle Words

1. SHOW
2. HARE
3. GLOW
4. CARE
5. COME
6. PAIR
7. COOK
8. MIND
9. TORE
10. LINE

3.5 Practice

1. tree, bush
2. school, classroom
3. sheep, horse
4. mouse, badger
5. gentleman, boy
6. scared, frightened
7. dear, expensive
8. rubbish, litter
9. thick, wide
10. thin, slim
11. rude, polite
12. sleep, awake
13. entree, dessert
14. stop, start
15. old, young
16. DEAR
17. RACK
18. READ
19. CLIP
20. BAND

4.1 Can(not) be made

1. fare
2. prod
3. lone
4. went
5. hail
6. dial
7. rain
8. gong
9. drum
10. sent

4.2 Compound Words

1. pass, port
2. sand, paper
3. eye, lid
4. hand, shake
5. finger, print
6. so, on
7. fat, her
8. sud, den
9. butter, fly
10. check, up

4.3 Rearranging Words

1. ducks
2. care
3. fear
4. clip
5. flag
6. plum
7. some
8. rise
9. tail
10. rose
11. dim
12. fun
13. sow
14. gel
15. noun
16. fuel
17. rust
18. rant
19. find
20. plum

4.4 Transferring letters

1. (c) at, chose
2. (r) beak, tear
3. (h) cook, hair
4. (f) lock, fair
5. (e) not, ripe
6. (t) meal, part
7. (u) lot, menu
8. (p) seed, spell
9. (h) cat, champ
10. (c) lie, scale

4.5 Practice

1. hurt
2. ever
3. lout
4. bale
5. lion
6. in, to
7. stop, watch
8. foot, print
9. sun, day
10. beet, root
11. liner
12. bleak
13. ache
14. lady
15. last
16. (u) for, unit
17. (s) tone, stag
18. (l) fare, cold or clod
19. (a) far, read
20. (c) hat, cloud

5.1 Simple Codes

1. 347227
2. REGION
3. 3257
4. 4871
5. DARE
6. NOTE
7. HBOEL
8. LEAF
9. DOOR
10. LPSME

5.2 Adding Codes

1. ANNJ
2. PLAY
3. BSVC
4. APNUM
5. DRINK
6. SSOJ
7. QQTV
8. DOOR
9. DOES
10. PKEG

5.3 Number Codes

1. 18 11 14 22
2. TALK
3. 16 25 7 12
4. 8 8 23 4
5. TOLD
6. DUST
7. 10 17 4 11
8. TIME
9. LOSE
10. 12 L 14 M

5.4 Alphabet Reflections

1. H V M W
2. WIND
3. S F I G
4. S R E V
5. EXAM
6. FALL
7. X Z O U
8. PENS
9. THIS
10. K O Z B

5.5 Practice

1. S B J O
2. THANK
3. U G L B M U
4. T J R I X
5. AIRCRAFT
6. SHARK
7. I T X W Q O
8. FIRST
9. FRIEND
10. K M T G C
11. 26 2 13 21 14
12. OUTFIT
13. 7 Q 19 G 20 V
14. RIDER
15. U 7 B 18 F
16. GRASS
17. H J F Z I V
18. TASTE
19. TAIL
20. T I V Z G

6.1 Links

1. 6
2. 2
3. 3
4. 5
5. 10
6. 5
7. 15
8. 2
9. 2
10. 4
11. 11
12. 20
13. 71
14. 9
15. 36
16. 14
17. 10
18. 30
19. 6
20. 10

6.2 Substitution

1. 4
2. 10
3. 4
4. 4
5. 8
6. D
7. C
8. A
9. C
10. E

6.3 Equalities

1. 2
2. 10
3. 4
4. 7
5. 5
6. 9
7. 3
8. 8
9. 2
10. 4

6.4 Number Sequences

1. 13
2. 10
3. 32
4. 28
5. 250
6. 4
7. 10
8. 5
9. 16
10. 6

6.5 Practice

1. 24
2. 3
3. 20
4. 4
5. 30
6. C
7. E
8. C
9. A
10. D
11. 27
12. 5
13. 1
14. 4
15. 6
16. 48
17. 15
18. 25
19. 12
20. 8

7.1 Mixed up Codes

1. 2163
2. FEAR
3. 6153
4. 7513
5. TENT
6. 36751
7. 3175
8. FARE
9. RATS
10. 4231

7.2 Go With Two Groups

1. staff
2. minute
3. rose
4. land
5. stone
6. mole
7. close
8. pound
9. book
10. flat

7.3 Word Analogies

1. second, silver
2. fresh, polluted
3. foal, cub
4. whine, deer
5. pride, school
6. right, no
7. milk, paper
8. talk, firm
9. meat, bread
10. nail, staple

7.4 Belonging

1. second
2. lungs
3. Athens
4. newsagent
5. teenager
6. electrician
7. taxi
8. whole
9. ash
10. projector

7.5 Practice

1. 9354
2. STEW
3. WINNER
4. 4745
5. HEARTH
6. 2534
7. watch
8. bear
9. nail
10. left
11. drank, found
12. ram, stag
13. lose, demolish
14. flakes, drops
15. pain, way
16. cup
17. hundred
18. double bass
19. square
20. bean

8.1 What number?

1. 40
2. 17
3. Joanna and Alison
4. 600
5. 10
6. Baljeet
7. 5
8. 7
9. 107
10. 3

8.2 What Time?

1. January
2. 8:09a.m.
3. 10:15p.m.
4. 1:00a.m.
5. 80 minutes
6. December
7. 50 minutes
8. 18:00
9. 28
10. 120 years

8.3 Can(not) be True

1. A
2. B
3. D
4. B
5. D
6. B
7. C
8. D
9. D
10. C

8.4 Sorting Info

1. Nasir
2. Hamza
3. Kane
4. D
5. Ola
6. C
7. A
8. Ryszard
9. Townville
10. 3

8.5 Practice

1. B
2. French
3. Terrence
4. Priyanka
5. Winston
6. D
7. Julian, Ida
8. 6 minutes
9. 14:42
10. D

9.1 Comprehension

1. C
2. B
3. A
4. A
5. C
6. D
7. C
8. C
9. B
10. B

9.2 Cloze

1. teacher, student, how
2. orbits, sun, year
3. seed, of, oak
4. goes, is, closed
5. sells, milk, goats
6. become, for, first
7. excited, his, weeks
8. are, become, not
9. capital, Scotland, Edinburgh
10. accident, yesterday, jam

9.3 Two Words Between

1. CARE / CORE or FARE
2. FACE / FACT
3. BENT / BEAT
4. LOST / LOSE
5. SLOT / PLOT or SLOP
6. FLAP / FLAW / FLOP
7. ROSE / ROLE
8. CHAT / COAT
9. SALE / BALE
10. GRAND / GLAND or BRAND

9.4 Extra Words

1. dream
2. drink
3. is
4. reads
5. primitive
6. was
7. the
8. stars
9. an
10. will

9.5 Practice

1. D
2. A
3. B
4. B
5. D
6. electrician, wired, sold
7. four, sides, no
8. carbon dioxide, and oxygen
9. animals, active, night
10. friction, force, opposes
11. SHOP / SHIP
12. FILL / SILL
13. ALONG / ALONE
14. SHORE / CHORE
15. STEP / STOP
16. treats
17. is
18. lots
19. moon
20. low

10.1 Crossword Grids

1.

S	H	O	R	T
T				R
A	B	O	D	E
R				A
T	Y	P	E	D

2.

F	R	O	W	N
E				O
A	D	O	P	T
S				C
T	O	U	G	H

3.

T	O	R	C	H
R				O
U	R	B	A	N
T				E
H	U	R	R	Y

4.

S	H	O	R	E
T				X
R	I	N	S	E
A				R
Y	E	A	S	T

5.

C	H	A	N	T
R				R
E	X	T	R	A
S				I
T	A	K	E	N

6.

C	L	O	V	E
A		A		D
B		S		G
I		I		E
N	O	S	E	S

7.

E	V	E	R	Y
T		L		A
H		D	E	W
O		E		N
S	O	R	T	S

8.

A	T	E
N	O	W
T	E	E

9

H	A	U	L
A	C	R	E
U	R	G	E
L	E	E	K

10.

L	E	A	S	T
A	H	I		O
K		S	O	W
E		L		E
S	P	E	A	R

10.2 Definitions

1. donation
2. rhombus
3. legible
4. gratitude
5. focus
6. slack
7. scrawl
8. errand
9. elaborate
10. current

10.3 Letters Missing

1. ACK
2. MIN
3. NESD or DNES
4. ICE
5. CRE
6. ETA
7. DUS
8. HOD
9. IMP
10. EAL

10.4 Scrabble Words

1. girl
2. tin
3. ring
4. age
5. gale
6. lie
7. live
8. bled
9. dive
10. slide

10.5 Practice

1.

S	E	A
H	A	D
E	R	A

2.

S	O	L	I	D
A				A
F	I	V	E	R
E				E
R	A	P	I	D

3.

S	A	B	R	E
T		A		M
O		S	E	A
N		I		I
E	X	C	E	L

4.

G	E	R	M	S
E		E		C
N		L	E	A
U		A		L
S	T	Y	L	E

5.

S	P	R	E	A	D
P	I	E	R	C	E
R	E	G	R	E	T
E	R	R	A	T	A
A	C	E	T	I	C
D	E	T	A	C	H

6. Will
7. Trilogy
8. Tsunami
9. Hospitable
10. Brave
11. HOPP
12. ICE
13. ESE
14. ECT
15. CAS
16. scent
17. ten
18. tense
19. fine
20. sent

11.1 Two Letters

1. ZE
2. VE
3. TH
4. ST
5. TE
6. OW
7. GE
8. AM
9. ED
10. IT

11.2 Anagrams

1. computer
2. silent
3. elephants
4. prescribed
5. limestone
6. average
7. circus
8. century
9. justify
10. tomorrow

11.3 Word in Front

1. over
2. for
3. out
4. sun
5. back
6. foot
7. pass
8. fire
9. head
10. sand

11.4 Word Structure

1. ought, tough
2. start, tarts
3. thin, hint
4. towel
5. frost
6. wasps
7. kayak
8. minim
9. rough, stuff
10. cheque, wreck

11.5 Practice

1. CH
2. CE
3. RE
4. SH
5. AN
6. rubbish
7. clouds
8. orchestra
9. listen
10. assortment
11. up
12. soft
13. hand
14. sea
15. post
16. easel, lease
17. night, thing
18. flesh, shelf
19. shrub, brush
20. racecar

Printed in Great Britain
by Amazon

27609524R00079